# BACK TO JERUSALEM

回耶路撒冷

Billy,

"Look to the rock from
which you were cut and
to the quarry from which
you were hewn. ISA 51:16.

May the Lord use this
book to see God's heart for
the nations in a NEW way

Together, Serving in mission

Bill Harding IV

*Asia is the greatest theater of the Twentieth Century. It is going to witness the mightiest movements, politically, socially, educationally, and spiritually, of any continent of the world. It may be questioned whether any other continent, in any other century, has had take place upon it what we shall see unfold upon the Asiatic continent, even in our own generation. . . . We shall witness the greatest triumphs of Christianity. . . .*

*China has impressed me more than any other nation I have visited. . . . The Chinese have the characteristics of the great races of the world: industry, frugality, patience, tenacity, great physical vigor, great intellectual power, independence, and conservatism. These are the great qualities which have marked off the great races of the world, and the Chinese possess them in a wonderful degree. . . .*

*We must first evangelize the young men, and secondly, make them an evangelizing force. . . . It is beyond all question that the one thing, and the only thing, that can uplift and regenerate China is the Gospel of Christ. What people have such remarkable staying power, such large capacity for work, such patient endurances of hardship and suffering! Surely God has a special purpose in preserving the integrity of this nation for four thousand years. . . . The qualities which have made the Chinese such efficient agents of evil will make them, under the transforming, directing, and energizing power of the Holy Spirit, one of the mightiest forces for the upbuilding of the kingdom of God. Their influence is destined to be increasingly felt far beyond the limits of the Middle Kingdom.*

*The more we reflect on the strong traits of this people, the more we are impressed with what Napoleon said:"When China is moved it will change the face of the globe."*

John R. Mott,
"When China is Moved it Will Change the Face of the Globe,"
*China's Millions*, April 1902

# BACK TO JERUSALEM

Three Chinese
Vision to (

Broth(

**Gabriel**
Publishing

This edition copyright © 2003 by Piquant
PO Box 83, Carlisle, CA3 9GR, United Kingdom
E-mail: info@piquant.net or visit www.piquant.net

ISBN 1-884543-89-8

Published in the United States of America by Gabriel Resources
129 Mobilization Drive, Waynesboro, GA, 30830, USA
706-554-5827
E-mail: gabriel@omlit.om.org

Cover design: ProjectLuz
Cover photograph: Revival Christian Church, Hong Kong. Used with
permission.

# Contents

# Maps and Photographs

## Maps

## Photographs *(see the photo insert)*

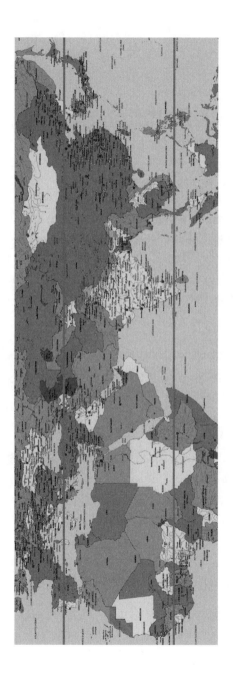

Map 1. The 10/40 window. The bold lines mark the area inhabited by more than 90% of the world's remaining unreached people groups and all fifty of the world's least evangelized countries. These countries are the focus of the Back to Jerusalem movement.

# Preface

*The Back to Jerusalem vision is something that thousands of
Chinese Christians are willing to die for. At the very least, we
ought to find out why.*

I first heard talk about the Back to Jerusalem movement after
arriving in China in the 1980s. One or two preachers mentioned it
in their sermons, but I didn't have a clue what it meant. I presumed
that the Chinese church wanted to evangelize Jerusalem, which I
found mildly interesting, but not enough to distract me from my
missionary endeavors!

Years later, as the Lord graciously opened doors of relationship
with house church leaders from different parts of China, I came to
realize that Back to Jerusalem was a passion for many of them. They
prayed about it daily, dreamed about it, and spoke about it over
breakfast, lunch and dinner. The Back to Jerusalem vision is not a
trivial matter for many Christian leaders, but the driving force of
their lives and ministries. Many feel it is the destiny to which God
has called the Chinese church, the very reason they exist!

Knowing that Christian leaders in China walk closely with the
Lord and are constantly guided by his word and the Holy Spirit, I
thought it would be worth learning all I could about the Back to
Jerusalem movement in order to better understand what it is all
about. The more I learned from history and from listening to the
house church leaders, the more this vision filled my own heart, until
my family and I now consider that the rest of our lives could not
be better spent than in serving the Chinese church and the Back to
Jerusalem vision.

The first thing I came to understand was that Back to Jerusalem
does *not* mean that the Chinese want to rush to Jerusalem with the
gospel. Their vision is much larger than that. Nor is Back to Jerusalem
some kind of end-times theory. The Chinese church has no plans to

rush to Israel to usher in the return of Christ. Rather, it refers to a call from God for the Chinese church to preach the gospel and establish fellowships of believers in all the countries, cities, towns, and ethnic groups *between* China and Jerusalem. This is no small task, for within those regions lie the three largest spiritual strongholds that have yet to be conquered by the gospel: the giants of Islam, Buddhism, and Hinduism.

In recent years many Christians have heard of the 10/40 window, referring to the areas of the world that lie between 10 degrees and 40 degrees north of the Equator. All fifty of the world's least-Christian and least-evangelized countries are located within this region! It contains more than 90 percent of the unreached people groups in the world—more than five thousand tribes and ethnolinguistic groups with little or no gospel witness.

Although few of China's Christians have ever heard of the 10/40 window, they, too, have a vision of taking the good news into those nations that have remained in spiritual darkness for so long.

\*   \*   \*

In 2002 a number of house church leaders from various church networks expressed their frustration at the lack of understanding of the Back to Jerusalem vision among Christians around the world. They asked if a book could be produced that explains the history and background of the movement; one that communicates the passion China's Christians have for Back to Jerusalem and reveals some of the plans and strategies the Lord has given the Chinese church as they start to see this dream become a reality.

The book you hold in your hands is the result of their desire. My role has merely been to listen to them and to give form to the message they wished to communicate to you but could not because of their limited knowledge of English. The voices behind this book are those of three leading house church figures, Brother Yun, Peter Xu Yongze, and Enoch Wang. These three men are widely known throughout the church in China, and two of them are already living outside China for the purpose of training Back to Jerusalem missionaries and facilitating their work.

These men of God speak from deep personal experience. Between them they have spent a total of almost forty years in prison for their faith, and through their sufferings have learned much about God's character and his work. In chapters 5 to 7, each in turn will tell his story and describe the vision for Back to Jerusalem. I know that their views are representative of those of hundreds of other house church leaders I have had the privilege to meet.

As you read these pages, please remember that the Back to Jerusalem movement is not merely wishful thinking by a few fanatical Christians. It is something that is *already* happening! The first team of thirty-nine Chinese missionaries departed China in March 2000 for a neighboring Buddhist country. They were the small trickle signalling a great flood to come. Few people around the world knew of this event, but their going was the result of years of prayer and planning. On that day China once again became an active participant in worldwide mission. Today there are hundreds of Chinese missionaries working outside China in the Middle East, North Africa, Central Asia, the Indian subcontinent, and Southeast Asia. Thousands more are in training, learning languages such as Arabic and English that will be put to use on the mission field.

During the training and orientation for those first pioneers, each was asked to give their testimony. Many tears flowed as they told their stories. All had suffered much for the gospel in China. Most had been arrested, imprisoned, beaten, and tortured because of their testimony for Jesus Christ. They had all faced extreme hardship, separation from their families, forced starvation, sleepless nights, and perils on every side. All had faithfully preached the gospel throughout China for years, establishing churches and seeing more of God's power manifested through their ministries each month than most Christians see during their lifetimes.

According to normal Western missionary methods, these workers were unqualified. None had ever attended a seminary and most would think that a theological degree is something found on a thermometer! Yet they had received training from God that is far more important than what can be learned in a classroom, an experiential training in the furnace of affliction. Brother Yun, one of the leading figures in the Back to Jerusalem movement, comments:

> Sometimes Western visitors come to China and ask the house church leaders what seminary they attended. We reply, jokingly yet with underlying seriousness, that we have been trained in the Holy Spirit Personal Devotion Bible School (prison) for many years.

Sometimes our Western friends don't understand what we mean because they then ask, "What materials do you use in this Bible school?" We reply, "Our only materials are the foot chains that bind us and the leather whips that bruise us."

In this prison seminary, we have learned many valuable lessons about the Lord that we could never have learned from a book. We've come to know God in a deeper way. We understand his goodness and his loving faithfulness to us.[1]

The Back to Jerusalem missionaries have little money, no fundraising plans, no newsletter mailing lists, or glossy magazines. Few have ever used a computer or know what it means to download information from the Internet. They don't know much about making money, but they do know how to make disciples for Jesus. They have no investment portfolios, but they already have a rich inheritance stored up in heaven.

When offerings are received during house church meetings in China, evangelists sometimes find they have absolutely nothing to put into the bag. So they literally step into the offering bag themselves and unconditionally offer their whole lives as a living sacrifice to the service of God.

The Chinese church doesn't draw up presumptuous plans but has learned to wait on the Lord and listen to his instructions before moving forward. These men and women know God, his all-sufficiency, and his matchless grace and power. They are not only going out into the world with a message, they are living messages. They are absolutely nothing in the eyes of the world, but are sharp arrows in the hands of God.

Like the Apostle Paul, the Chinese church has heard the words of Jesus, *"My grace is sufficient for you, for my power is made perfect in weakness"* (2 Cor. 12:9). And like Paul, the Chinese say with great assurance, *"That is why, for Christ's sake, I delight in weaknesses, in insults, in hardships, in persecutions, in difficulties. For when I am weak, then I am strong"* (2 Cor. 12:10).

Oswald Chambers once wrote, "If you give God the right to yourself, He will make a holy experiment out of you. God's experiments always succeed." God has been conducting a lot of experiments in China, and he is ready to show the results to the world.

God never changes. While we are looking for better methods and stronger men and women, God is looking for weak vessels with no confidence in their own abilities. He does this so that his work will be done his way and so that all the glory will go to Jesus Christ. God always chooses *"the foolish things of the world to shame the wise; God chose the weak things of the world to shame the strong. He chose the lowly things of this world and the despised things—and the things that are not—to nullify the things that are, so that no one may boast before him"* (1 Cor. 1:27–29).

As the Back to Jerusalem vision unfolds, you may start to hear reports of Muslims, Hindus, and Buddhists coming to Christ in places where the gospel has long struggled to make an impact. When this happens, don't be amazed at the Chinese Christians, they are just sinners saved by grace and undeserving of any attention. Rather, be amazed at the wisdom and manifest beauty of God's plan. *"For the foolishness of God is wiser than man's wisdom, and the weakness of God is stronger than man's strength"* (1 Cor. 1:25).

In the next chapter, I present a brief overview of the history of the church in China and of its position today. In the rest of the book, three Chinese church leaders share their vision for taking the gospel back to Jerusalem.

I hope you will be encouraged and challenged by the Back to Jerusalem vision, and moved to prayer and involvement in the fulfilment of the Great Commission in these last days, until *"the kingdom of the world has become the kingdom of our Lord and of his Christ, and he will reign for ever and ever"* (Rev. 11:15).

Paul Hattaway

# 1

# The Church in China

*Look at the nations and watch—and be utterly amazed. For I am going to do something in your days that you would not believe, even if you were told.*

*— Habakkuk 1:5*

Back to Jerusalem represents the present and future vision of the twenty-first-century Chinese church. To fully understand and appreciate what it means to them, we must first understand the past. In this chapter we give a quick overview of God's involvement with China throughout history and explain how China's church evolved to the place where many leaders today consider Back to Jerusalem the primary goal and ultimate reward of their labours. In fact, many Christians believe the fifty years of persecution they have endured has not been the plan of Satan to destroy the church in China as much as it has been God's plan to refine, train, and equip them to complete the Back to Jerusalem vision.

Over the past five decades something remarkable has started to take place throughout the length and breadth of China: the emergence of a viable New Testament Christianity. Few secular sources report the unfolding of this dramatic event, which has the potential to change the entire social and moral structure of the nation if it continues unabated.

At the dawn of the new millennium, I had the privilege of meeting with a number of Chinese house church leaders. These men and women were unremarkable in themselves. Most came from simple farming backgrounds, yet to be in their presence was an exhilarating experience. I was aware—as many Christians around the world are—that China has been experiencing a revival of Christianity in recent decades that has had an impact on many parts of their vast nation. I had read reports of mass conversions, secret baptisms, and brutal persecution.

During that special meeting the leaders of each house church network, or "family", testified about what God was doing in their

1

midst and reported on the growth their churches were experiencing. They had been asked some time before to research the number of church fellowships and believers in their networks as accurately as possible. The top leaders asked their provincial and regional leaders to submit reports. These people then gathered the statistics from grassroots house church leaders, who operate at the city and county level.

The information was then collated by the top leaders, who were gathered at the special meeting. The combined total membership of the house church networks present at the meeting came to 58 million people, while the net growth rate of each church group was reported to be between 12.5 per cent and 17.5 per cent per year. Some experts estimate that thirty thousand Chinese are coming to Christ each day, which works out to more than ten million new believers annually.

Even though the number of conversions in China today does not yet match the birth rate (approximately 55,000 babies are born each day), at the present rate of growth the church in China will soon be expanding at a faster numerical rate than the country as a whole.

As I chatted with these leaders, I learned more of their zeal, love and sacrificial commitment to the cause of Christ. These were not merely believers, they were disciples of Jesus. They did not preach a "ticket to heaven" gospel, they preached and demonstrated the reality of the kingdom of God. They had paid a great price for their witness. Every single Christian leader in the meeting had spent time in prison, and many had been subjected to severe torture, humiliation, and deprivation. You would never know it, however, as they were the most joyful and sincere people you could ever hope to meet. Their joy was not a superficial emotion but a reality that came from deep within their souls—a supernatural kind of joy that only those who have truly enthroned Jesus Christ as the Master and Lover of their souls can ever experience.

One lunch time I asked several church leaders how many Christians they thought there would be in China in twenty or thirty years time if the gospel continued to blaze its way through the nation as it had been doing for the previous decade. "Two hundred million believers?" I asked with a smile on my face. "Three hundred million?"

The Chinese brothers didn't answer. They understood my

question, but didn't understand my lack of faith! After repeating the question, one leader, with a puzzled look on his face, said, "Of course in twenty or thirty years *all* of China will know the Lord!"

I have learned not to impose my limited Western thinking on the Chinese church. They believe that part of their mandate from God is to completely evangelize their whole nation and to make China "the first truly born-again Christian country in Asia."

Don't be surprised if they succeed.

## An Ancient Link to God

*He has made everything beautiful in his time. He has also set eternity in the hearts of men; yet they cannot fathom what God has done from beginning to end.*

— *Ecclesiastes 3:11*

In the decades after missionaries started to flood into China, diligent study of Chinese archives and historic literature uncovered some remarkable facts from China's distant past. In addition to legends handed down since the dawn of time about Creation, a worldwide flood, and a family who survived by finding refuge inside a large boat, there is considerable evidence pointing to ancient China having had a deep reverence for the Creator God. The Creator was never represented by an image or idol. The ancient Chinese believed that he reigned supreme over the affairs of mankind. Indeed, the original meaning of many written Chinese characters has been shown to reveal biblical stories and principles.[2]

For centuries the Chinese emperor offered annual sacrifices to *Shangdi*, the Heavenly Emperor. Shangdi is the name Chinese Protestants still use for God. The annual prayer recited by the emperor included the following fascinating words:

Of old in the beginning, there was great chaos, without form and dark. The five elements [planets] had not begun to evolve, nor the sun and moon to shine. In the midst thereof there existed neither form nor sound. You, O Spiritual Sovereign, came forth in your presidency, and first did divide the grosser part from the purer. You made heaven; You made earth; You made man. All things with their reproducing power got their being. . . .

To thee, O mysteriously-working Maker, I look up in thought. . . . With the great ceremonies I reverently honor Thee. Thy servant, I am but a reed or willow; my heart is but that of an ant; yet have I received Thy favouring decree, appointing me to the government of the empire. I deeply cherish a sense of my ignorance and blindness, and am afraid, lest I prove unworthy of Thy great favors. Therefore will I observe all the rules and statutes, striving, insignificant as I am, to discharge my loyal duty. For distant here, I look up to Thy heavenly palace. Come in Thy precious chariot to the altar. Thy servant, I bow my head to the earth reverently, expecting Thine abundant grace. . . . O that Thou wouldest vouchsafe to accept our offerings, and regard us, while thus we worship Thee, whose goodness is inexhaustible![3]

May the present generation of Chinese leaders come to possess the same humility and reverence for God as their predecessors!

It seems clear that world's most populous nation had a special place in God's purposes in the distant past. Could it be that China also has an important role to play for God's kingdom in these last days?

Although firm evidence first dates the arrival of Christianity in China to the Nestorians in A.D. 635, many Christians in China believe that at least one of the Magi who visited the infant Jesus came from China. This belief is based on anecdotal evidence about a man named Liu Shang, who was the chief astrologer at the court of the Han rulers at the time of Christ's birth. Liu disappeared for two years after discovering a new star the Chinese called the "king star." It was believed that a king was born whenever this star appeared. The Chinese possessed advanced astronomy at the time, and Liu Shang could have traveled the Silk Road, which was already in use. A journey from China to Jerusalem would have taken between one and two years, and it is interesting to note that the gospel account states that King Herod *"gave orders to kill all the boys in Bethlehem and its vicinity who were two years old and under, in accordance with the time he had learned from the Magi"* (Matt. 2:16).

Although it is impossible to prove this story, a recent startling discovery suggests that Christianity in China could date back almost as far as the birth of the New Testament church itself. In 2002 Wang Weifang, a 74-year-old professor of theology and a standing member of the China Christian Council, discovered a batch of stone carvings in the Xuzhou Museum in Jiangsu Province:

Wang was greatly surprised by some stone engravings demonstrating the Bible stories and designs of early Christian times. Further studies showed that some of these engravings were made in A.D. 86, or the third year under the reign of Emperor Yuanhe of the Eastern Han Dynasty. . . . Wang compared the designs on them with that of the Bible, composed of fish, birds, and animals demonstrating how God created the earth.

Designs on these ancient stones displayed the artistic style of early Christian times found in Iraq and the Middle East area while bearing the characteristics of China's Eastern Han times.

The stone carvings, being important funeral objects, are mainly found in four cities, and Xuzhou is one of them. It is reported that by now more than 20 intact Han tombs have been found, from which nearly 500 pieces of engraved stones were discovered.[4]

# The Missionary Era

In the more modern era, Catholic missionaries beat Protestants to China by more than five hundred years, displaying tremendous perseverance and courage as they battled to establish a beachhead on Chinese soil. Protestant missionaries first made an appearance when Englishman Robert Morrison's boat docked in Guangzhou in September 1807.

During the voyage, the captain of the ship asked Morrison, "Do you really expect to make an impression on the idolatry of the great Chinese empire?" The Protestant pioneer gave his now famous reply, "No, sir. But I expect God will."

He has!

Progress was slow for Morrison. Seven years after his arrival he baptized his first convert "at a stream of water issuing from the foot of a lofty hill, far away from human observation. . . . May he be the first-fruits of a great harvest, one of millions who shall believe!"[5]

In the following decades the missionary enterprise in China grew exponentially. Most of the missionaries were deeply consecrated to God, willing to die for the gospel. One man of faith said, "I expect to die in heathen China, but I expect to rise in Christian China."[6] His expectation looks more and more likely to be fulfilled.

The number of Chinese converts from the 150 years of Protestant missionary enterprise was not huge, but a solid foundation was laid for future developments.

Undoubtedly the most famous of the missionaries was James Hudson Taylor, the founder of the non-denominational China Inland Mission. He is fondly remembered by house church leaders in China today. One of the key figures in the Back to Jerusalem movement, Peter Xu Yongze, talks about the deep respect he has for Taylor:

> The vision of the house churches in China today is not only to saturate our own country with the life and presence of the Lord Jesus Christ, but also to impact all the remaining Muslim, Buddhist and Hindu nations with the gospel. This is why we are so thankful for the impact Hudson Taylor made on our country. His example was one of single-minded passion to see God's kingdom come. Like a mighty soldier he marched into pioneer areas where the Name of Jesus Christ had never been uttered before.
>
> Today the house churches in China have caught that same vision. It is as though Hudson Taylor handed a flaming torch to the Chinese church and asked us to continue the race towards the finish line.

Although most books about Hudson Taylor's ministry tend to focus on Western missionary methods, a careful examination of the work of the China Inland Mission reveals that these missionaries increasingly saw their role as being trainers and facilitators of local Chinese Christian leaders. Simply speaking, it was their Chinese co-workers who did most of the front-line work, while the Western missionaries increasingly supported and encouraged their efforts from the background. Early in his career, Taylor wrote:

> The harvest here is indeed great, and the laborers are few and imperfectly fitted for such a work. And yet grace can make a few feeble instruments the means of accomplishing great things – things greater than even we can conceive.[7]

Decades later there was a clear shift in Taylor's strategy as he realized that the Chinese church would never fully grow and mature as long as missionaries remained in leadership and decision-making positions within the Body of Christ. Note the change of emphasis in the following passage:

> I look upon foreign missionaries as the scaffolding around a rising building. The sooner it can be dispensed with, the better; or rather, the sooner it can be transferred to other places, to serve the same temporary use, the better.[8]

Many years later the son of Hudson Taylor summarized his father's ministry in this way:

> For threescore years and ten, my father, Mr. Hudson Taylor, and his successors, and the members of the China Inland Mission, with many other missionaries, have realized that China must be evangelized by Chinese Christians. Now, thank God, it is being so evangelized more than ever before. A good beginning has been made. . . . These devoted, consecrated workers are ready for sacrifice and hardship, at times great hardship, if only Christ may see of the travail of His soul and be satisfied. They love Him who died for them, and wish, at all costs, to live for Him.[9]

In an ethnocentric and proud nation like China, an effective indigenous strategy was essential. The Chinese masses would never embrace a "foreigner's religion." The appearance and structure of Christianity had to change before the Chinese would accept it. One Chinese onlooker in the 1890s listened to a powerful sermon from a local evangelist. He made the following insightful comment:

> Once a forest was told that a load of axe-heads had come to cut it down. "It doesn't matter in the least," said the forest, "they will never succeed by themselves." When, however, it heard that some of its own branches had become handles to the axe-heads, it said, "Now we have no chance."

> So as long as we only had foreigners to deal with, we were safe, but now that everywhere our own countrymen are enlisted on that side, certainly Christianity will flourish and conquer us.[10]

Alas, many missionary organizations did not share Hudson Taylor's insights, and continued to act like parents to the fledgling Chinese church. Not surprisingly, China continued to view Christianity as a Western religion and its Chinese adherents as traitors and slaves of their Western masters. A common Chinese saying at the time was "One more Chinese Christian equals one less Chinese."

The 1920s were "a high-water mark for the missionary enterprise in China."[11] More than 10,000 foreign missionaries were scattered throughout the land. Many were fully committed, sacrificial Christians and God used them in different ways, but once the church had taken root their role clearly should have been to step aside and let the Chinese lead and direct their own congregations.

One of the most telling indictments of the missionary enterprise in the early twentieth century is not found in any words or sermons but in a picture taken at a key conference held in 1907 at the Martyr's Memorial Hall in Shanghai. The meeting was called to plan for the future of Christianity in China, yet close inspection of the attendees reveals a room full of black-suited Western missionaries. Shockingly, a mere handful of Chinese pastors felt comfortable enough to attend this key meeting to determine the future of the Chinese church. They were largely lost among the eight hundred foreign delegates to the meeting. The 1907 meeting was just one of a series of conferences in Shanghai dating back to 1877, all of which were dominated by the foreign missionary force.

The church in China continued to grow slowly during the missionary era, but not at the pace or in the form necessary for the world's largest nation to experience Christ's salvation in the way God wanted them to. Christians remained marginalized within Chinese society. The church with all its Western trappings had erected physical, spiritual, and cultural walls between the Chinese Christians and the unsaved millions surrounding them.

Towards the close of the nineteenth century, missionary zeal in Britain started to wane and many church leaders wanted to forget about evangelizing the world and to confine their Christian work to their home parishes. One Christian statistician announced that the work of foreign missionaries in China had been an abject failure. His research indicated that at the rate the gospel was advancing, it would take another twenty-seven thousand years for the conversion rate in China to draw level with the birth rate! It was estimated that even if the population of China remained static, it would take another 1,680,000 years to convert them![12]

God, however, had other ideas. He would not allow the Chinese masses to languish in their sin and spiritual darkness while the glorious news of the victory of his beloved Son on the cross remained unheralded in the world's largest nation.

# The Start of Persecution and Revival

*For it has been granted to you on behalf of Christ not only to believe on him, but also to suffer for him.*
                                                    *— Philippians 1:29*

On October 1, 1949, Mao Zedong climbed a podium in Beijing's Tiananmen Square and announced the birth of the People's Republic of China.

For the first few years the Communists stood back and watched the church. To the surprise of many Christians, things continued largely unchanged. Like a tiger stalking its prey, the government was waiting for the most opportune time to strike. And strike it did in the early 1950s, when persecution commenced in full fury. Hundreds of church leaders were arrested, taken away during the night. Many died and were never heard of again. Others were sent to prison labor camps where they suffered silently for decades before being released into a changed China that looked little like the one they had known.

G. Campbell Morgan once stated, "Satan's first choice is to cooperate with us. Persecution is only his second-best method." Sensing that the faithful believers in China would never compromise their inward trust in God, the devil and his evil forces tried to destroy the earthen vessels that contained this eternal treasure.

Many Christians who live in lands where physical persecution is not the norm struggle to understand the motivation of authorities who brutalize innocent believers simply because of their faith. There is no natural reason for persecution in China, especially as Christians are invariably the hardest working and most law-abiding citizens in the nation. Where there are large concentrations of Christians, the crime rate plummets to almost zero and there is peace and harmony between people who had previously been living in hostility. Yet the persecution continues.

There is an interesting story in an ancient Chinese book entitled *Han Feizi* about a man named Bian He who lived some five hundred years before Christ:

> Bian He found a large stone which was actually an unpolished piece of jade. He presented it to the emperor. The emperor saw nothing but a large stone, thought he was being tricked, and ordered Bian He's left foot to be chopped off. Bian He later sent the same present to the next emperor, who also saw only a stone and ordered his right foot to be chopped off. When a third emperor came to the throne, Bian He held his jade in his arms outside the emperor's palace and wept three days and three nights. The emperor sent someone to investigate,

then ordered the stone to be polished. Only then did they discover a beautiful jade inside it.

One day China (and many other nations) will discover that the Christians they torture, whom they suppose to be ignorant lumps of worthless stone, are actually the polished jewels sent by God to bring the blessing of Christ's salvation.

When persecution broke out against Christians throughout China in the 1950s there was no limit to the savagery displayed. Brother Yun recalls what took place when the persecution began:

> In just one city in China, Wenzhou in Zhejiang Province, 49 pastors were sent to prison labor camps near the Russian border in 1950. Many were given sentences of up to twenty years for their "crimes" of preaching the gospel. Of those 49 pastors, just one returned home. Forty-eight died in prison.
>
> In my home area of Nanyang believers were crucified on the walls of their churches for not denying Christ. Others were chained to vehicles and horses and dragged to their death.
>
> One pastor was bound and attached to a long rope. The authorities, enraged that the man of God would not deny his faith, used a makeshift crane to lift him high into the air. Before hundreds of witnesses, who had come to falsely accuse him of being a "counter-revolutionary", the pastor was asked one last time by his persecutors if he would recant. He shouted back, "No! I will never deny the Lord who saved me!" The rope was released and the pastor crashed to the ground below.
>
> Upon inspection, the tormentors discovered the pastor was not fully dead, so they raised him up into the air for a second time, dropping the rope to finish him off for good. In this life the pastor was dead, but he lives on in heaven with the reward of one who was faithful to the end.[13]

By 1953 almost all foreign missionaries had been expelled from China. Some refused to go willingly and were imprisoned for years. Many faithful missionaries who had served China with their lives now stood on the outside. Their work had suddenly been taken away from them. Reading missionary newsletters and magazines from the early 1950s, it is clear that few of the expelled missionaries could see the hand of God anywhere in their bitter experience. Most believed their expulsion was a victory for the devil, and many lamented the death of the Chinese church. The general consensus was that there was no way the fledgling believers left behind the Bamboo Curtain could survive the brutality of a totalitarian regime hell-bent on destroying Christianity once and for all. Several articles suggested that if and when China's doors ever reopened, the missionary enterprise would have to begin all over again.

They were wrong.

History and hindsight show that God's control of events is absolute. Although the persecution that occurred (and continues to occur) in China is unquestionably diabolical in nature, the evidence strongly suggests that God allowed it to happen so that his bride would be purified and equipped to bring more glory to her bridegroom.

One of the missionaries who had been expelled from China in the early 1950s was David Adeney of the Overseas Missionary Fellowship (formerly called the China Inland Mission). He later wrote:

> When all missionaries left China, the West was sometimes guilty of unbelieving pessimism. Seeing a weak and divided church, we felt we had failed. We knew many dedicated men and women and outstanding spiritual leaders. But could they, a tiny minority, stand against the mighty tide of a triumphant Communist ideology that proclaimed the "kingdom of man"—with no place for a crucified Savior? With no news of those we loved, our prayers became general and sporadic; most of us failed to enter into a continuous preserving prayer of faith. Now, as we hear of faithful witness in the midst of trial and great poverty, we feel rebuked for our lethargy, easy-going ways, affluence and lack of concern for the poor.[14]

The brutal persecution resulted in the church being stripped of all the external things associated with Christianity. Church buildings were confiscated and either demolished or used as warehouses, gymnasiums or storage facilities. Bibles and hymn books were burned, while almost the entire church leadership was removed. Unable to continue as they were used to, many Chinese Christians fell away. Some denied Christ and betrayed fellow believers. Those who decided to remain true to Jesus Christ found all of their religious props removed, leaving only one foundation that could not be moved—the Lord Jesus Christ himself.

Years later, China watchers were able to see how God had been in complete control of events in China throughout the years of silence. What most people believed to be a tragic defeat of the church turned out to be nothing less than a tremendous victory. It was presumed that the devil was destroying the church, when what was really happening was that God was pruning it so that it could produce more fruit. Jesus said, *"I am the true vine, and my Father is the gardener. He cuts off every branch in me that bears no fruit, while every branch that does bear fruit he prunes so that it will be even more fruitful."* (John 15:1–2).

Indeed, Chinese believers today joyfully explain that the Communist authorities, despite their efforts to demolish Christianity, actually paved the way for the rapid spread of the gospel. Before 1949 there was very little infrastructure in China, and linguistic, cultural, and geographic barriers greatly hindered the advance of the gospel. The Communists changed all this. Here are just some of the ways the policies of the government prepared the ground for the revival of Christianity:

- Much of China's idolatry was removed during the Cultural Revolution. Thousands of temples and idols were smashed, creating a spiritual void in the hearts of hundreds of millions of people.

- The government's attempts to remove God and deny the existence of the supernatural resulted in mass conversions to Christ when people personally experienced the reality of God and miracles.

- Train lines, roads and airports were constructed, enabling evangelists to easily travel to areas that were formerly inaccessible.

- Mandarin was adopted as the official language of China and is now used in all education and media. Formerly there were thousands of dialects that made communication of the gospel problematic.

- Large-scale literacy projects were undertaken, resulting in multitudes of people being able to read God's word for the first time.

- Control of the media resulted in a hunger and respect for the printed word. Christian organizations have taken advantage of this, printing tens of millions of Bibles and Christian books, while radio ministries were quick to broadcast the gospel by short-wave radio into China. Millions of Christians in China trace their salvation to radio ministry.

• During the excesses of the Cultural Revolution people were forced to denounce their wrongdoings and reform their lives. The "culture of confession" this created makes it much easier for people to repent and confess their sins to God when they hear the gospel.

It's little wonder that Christians in China today have a very deep realization of the sovereignty of God and his absolute control over human affairs! Despite living in the midst of a system dedicated to destroying them, Christians have learned to have no fear – not because they enjoy persecution and torture, but because they have met God and have been deeply transformed. They have experienced God's deep intimate love and come to personally know the truth of promises such as this one:

> *My sheep listen to my voice; I know them, and they follow me. I give them eternal life, and they shall never perish; no one can snatch them out of my hand. My Father, who has given them to me, is greater than all; no one can snatch them out of my Father's hand.* (John 10:27–29)

Estimates of the total number of Christians in China today vary, but I believe a figure of between 80 million and 100 million Protestants to be realistic, in addition to at least 12 million Catholic believers meeting in both registered churches and illegal house church gatherings.[15] Although these numbers still represent only a small minority of the 1,300 million souls inhabiting China today, the growth of the church is spectacular and unparalleled in Christian history when it is considered that there were only about 700,000 Protestants and three to four million Catholics in China at the time the Communists took power in 1949.

Surely the authorities in China have long been confused and amazed at how the church continues to grow and flourish despite their most brutal attempts to crush, seduce, and deceive believers. In their spiritual blindness they can't see they are fighting against a power far greater than their own, the power of Almighty God!

David Adeney was one former missionary astounded by what he found when China's iron doors slowly creaked open again in the late 1970s, after almost three decades of silence. While most expected to find the church had been completely obliterated, reports began filtering out that a great miracle had taken place! Somehow, in a way only God could do, the church in China had not merely survived the brutality of the past thirty years, but had actually grown and flourished! Amazing testimonies were received of how pastors were released after twenty years or more of imprisonment, and went home wondering whether they could find anyone who remembered their name. When they reached home, they found that not only had people been praying for them all those years, but their church fellowships had grown three, five or ten times as large as before their imprisonment!

In his book *China: The Church's Long March*,[16] Adeney joyfully documented the strengths the Chinese house churches had developed during their years of hardship. The following are some of the most important of these strengths:

1. *The house churches are indigenous.* They have cast off the trappings of the West and have developed their own forms of ministry. The dynamics flow from their freedom from institutional and traditional bondage.

2. *The house churches are rooted in family units.* They have become part of the Chinese social structure. The believing community is built up of little clusters of Christian families.

3. *The house churches are stripped of nonessentials.* Much that we associate with Christianity is not found in Chinese house churches today. Thus they are extremely flexible. One believer remarked, "In the past we blew trumpets and had large evangelistic campaigns. Some believed, but not great numbers. Now we have very little equipment . . . and many are coming to the Lord."

4. *The house churches emphasize the lordship of Christ.* Because Jesus is the head of his body, the church must place obedience to him above every other loyalty; it cannot accept control by any outside organization. The word of God is obeyed and every attempt to force unscriptural practices on the church is resisted.

5. *The house churches have confidence in the sovereignty of God.* When there was no hope from a human point of view, Christians in China saw God revealing his power and overruling in the history of their day.

6. *The house churches love the word of God.* They appreciate the value of the Scriptures and have sacrificed in order to obtain copies of the Bible. Their knowledge of the Lord has deepened as they have memorized and copied the word of God.

7. *The house churches are praying churches.* With no human support and surrounded by those seeking to destroy them, Christians were cast on God, and in simple faith expected God to hear their cry. Prayer was not only communion with God but also a way to share in the spiritual conflict.

8. *The house churches are caring and sharing churches.* A house church is a caring community in which Christians show love for one another and for their fellow countrymen. Such love creates a tremendous force for spontaneous evangelism.

9. *The house churches depend on lay leadership.* Because so many Chinese pastors were put into prison or labor camps, the house churches have had to depend on lay leaders. The leadership consists of people from various walks of life who spend much time going from church to church teaching and building up the faith of others.

10. *The house churches have been purified by suffering.* The church in China has learned firsthand that suffering is part of God's purpose in building his church. Suffering in the church has worked to purify it. Nominal Christianity could not have survived the tests of the Cultural Revolution. Because those who joined the church were aware that it was likely to mean suffering, their motivation was a genuine desire to know Jesus Christ.

11. *The house churches are zealous in evangelism.* No public preaching was allowed. People came to know Christ through the humble service of believers and through intimate contact between friends and family members. The main method of witness in China today is the personal lifestyle and behavior of Christians, accompanied by their proclamation of the gospel, often at great personal risk.

In the pages that follow, three Chinese house church leaders share the vision God has given them to take the gospel into the unevangelized Muslim, Buddhist, and Hindu nations and all the way "back to Jerusalem". These three men are representative of thousands of others with the same vision.

This is no small matter for the church in China. They consider it God's destiny for them, and they view the decades of torture, imprisonment, and slander they have experienced as God's training ground for their call to complete the Great Commission.

Back to Jerusalem is taken so seriously that thousands of people are willing to die for this vision. If it seems improbable or impossible to you, consider what the Chinese church has experienced over the past fifty years. They are used to seeing God do the impossible.

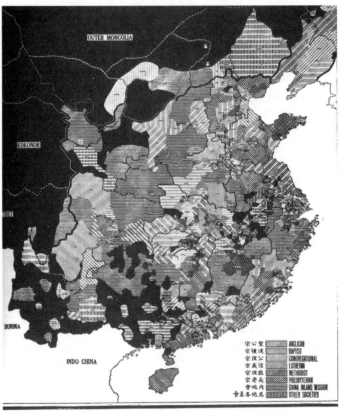

THE CHRISTIAN "PARTITIONMENT" OF CHINA. CAN CHINA BE MADE CHRISTIAN THIS WAY?

*The ill-starred map from the CCC survey volume,* The Christian Occupation of China, *presented to the new NCC in 1922. The caption is FJR's.*

Map 2. This 1922 map of China shows the various Western denominations working in different parts of the nation. A caption below the map asked, "Can China be made Christian this way?" History's clear answer was "No!" Through fifty years of persecution God pulled down denominational barriers, creating a more unified church that is more interested in winning souls than building their own churches. None of the Western denominations labelled on this map can be found among China's house churches today.

# 2

# The Roots of the Back to Jerusalem Movement*

*But you will receive power when the Holy Spirit comes on you, and you will be my witnesses in Jerusalem, and in all Judea and Samaria, and to the ends of the earth.*

— Acts 1:8

When we in China first read the above verse, we didn't know what "to the ends of the earth" meant. The way this Scripture is written makes it sound as if the earth is flat and it is possible for believers to reach the very end of the world, where it drops off into space! We prayed and meditated on this verse, asking God to show us what he means by it.

Gradually the Lord opened our minds to understand that what he was referring to was the geographic spread of the gospel throughout the world. When Jesus first gave this promise, he was standing on the Mount of Olives, just outside Jerusalem (see Acts 1:12). This hill is located on the east side of the old city, and at its highest point is approximately sixty meters (two hundred feet) higher than the temple area in Jerusalem. Therefore, when Jesus spoke the words of Acts 1:8 to his disciples, he was looking down on the city and his words showed a natural progression: *"You will be my witnesses in Jerusalem"* (the city down below where they were standing), *"Judea"* (the province to the west and northwest of Jerusalem), *"Samaria"* (the province to the north of Judea), *"and to the ends of the earth."*

Could it be that Jesus was showing his disciples that the fire of the gospel would first start to burn in Jerusalem, before spreading out into the countryside west and north of the city, then further into the lands bordering the Gentile world, and onward into those nations where God's name was not known?

---

* From this point on, the Chinese church leaders are the main authors of the text, with Paul Hattaway acting as their interpreter.

God helped the church to spread the gospel to the Gentiles. Even the location of Jerusalem was perfectly placed at the crossroads of Europe, Asia, and Africa. *"This is what the Sovereign Lord says: 'This is Jerusalem, which I have set in the centre of the nations, with countries all around her'"* (Ezek. 5:5).

The Book of Acts describes that this was exactly how the gospel did spread. After the Holy Spirit fell upon the believers with great power, Peter raised his voice and addressed the crowd: *"Fellow Jews and all of you who live in Jerusalem"* (Acts 2:14). The Holy Spirit anointed Peter with such authority that *"Those who accepted his message were baptized, and about three thousand were added to their number that day"* (Acts 2:41).

What a wonderful moment in history! The glorious gospel of Jesus Christ was just commencing its long and blessed journey throughout the world. Just as every parent longs to be present when his or her child takes their first step, surely all the angels watched and heaven stood still. The launch of the church brought life and salvation to three thousand people that very first day, in stark contrast to the introduction of the Old Testament Law, which had brought the death of three thousand people on its first day (see Exod. 32:27–28).

Those who had started to obey the Lord's command were doing a great job with stage one: Jerusalem. Indeed, soon the high priest complained to the followers of Jesus that they had *"filled Jerusalem with your teaching"* (Acts 5:28). Within weeks, the Bible states, *"the number of disciples in Jerusalem increased rapidly, and a large number of priests became obedient to the faith"* (Acts 6:7).

It seems to be an unfortunate characteristic of many Christians that when things are going well we like to stop, make ourselves comfortable, and enjoy our successes. The gospel had saturated Jerusalem, but the disciples were starting to forget the other stages of the Great Commission. To help them remember, the Lord provided some persecution! On the same day that Stephen became the first martyr of the church, *"a great persecution broke out against the church at Jerusalem, and all except the apostles were scattered throughout Judea and Samaria"* (Acts 8:1).

Philip was used mightily in Samaria, with miracles, signs and wonders accompanying his ministry, and many people came to faith in the recently ascended Christ. Soon after, God decided to reveal himself to one of the chief persecutors of the church, a man named Saul. The fourth stage in God's plan of world salvation would be implemented by the efforts of this man, who would come to be known as the Apostle Paul. Immediately after he dramatically met Jesus on the road to Damascus (the capital of Syria), the Lord said about Paul, *"This man is my chosen instrument to carry my name before the Gentiles and their kings"* (Acts 9:15).

The rest of the Book of Acts records how the fire of the gospel spread throughout the Roman world, to Rome itself, and to many areas along the Mediterranean coast. The Lord lovingly yet firmly helped the church obey his command, and in a short time the Jews said of Paul and Silas, *"These men who have caused trouble all over the world have now come here"* (Acts 17:6).

The words of Jesus in Luke 24:46–48 were being fulfilled: *"This is what is written: The Christ will suffer and rise from the dead on the third day, and repentance and forgiveness of sins will be preached in his name to all nations, beginning at Jerusalem. You are witnesses of these things."*

As we meditated on how the gospel had spread around the world, we saw that, generally speaking, the fire spread in a westward direction. From southern Europe it spread into central, northern, and western Europe. The fire also blazed into the southern Mediterranean countries in North Africa, giving birth to some of the great leaders of the early church such as Augustine (who came from present-day Algeria) and Tertullian (A.D. c. 155–220, who came from Tunisia). Tertullian's statement to the political leaders of his time still resonates among the Chinese house church Christians:

> Go zealously on, good presidents, you will stand higher with the people if you sacrifice the Christians at their wish, kill us, torture us, condemn us, grind us to dust; your injustice is the proof that we are innocent. . . . Nor does your cruelty, however exquisite, avail you; it is rather a temptation to us. The oftener we are mown down by you, the more in number we grow; the blood of Christians is seed.[17]

In China we understand what Tertullian meant. The government has come to view the house churches in the same way the Egyptians viewed the Israelites in captivity, *"the more they were oppressed, the more they multiplied and spread; so that the Egyptians came to dread the Israelites"* (Exod. 1:12).

We have numerous testimonies of powerful revivals that have

broken out in places where Christians have spilled their blood and endured many hardships for the gospel. In some areas where there is much opposition, it seems that God's children must suffer and bleed before demonic powers are broken and people can see the light of the gospel.

But, to return to the historical record, many centuries later, as adventurers and missionaries started exploring the world by ship, the fire of the gospel spread to central and southern Africa, to the Americas, to hundreds of islands in the South Pacific, to Australia, New Zealand, and parts of Asia on the Pacific Rim. Around the beginning of the twentieth century revival broke out in places like Korea, the Philippines, parts of eastern China, and Southeast Asia.

Of course there were many exceptions to this pattern. Indeed the Apostle Thomas is credited with having taken the gospel to India just years after he had touched the wounded hands of the resurrected Savior. But, generally speaking, we can see that the flame of the gospel has burned in a westward direction.

Beginning around thirty years ago, genuine and sustained revival came to the Chinese house churches. We found ourselves on the front-line of this worldwide fire of God's blessing, and many tens of millions of people have come to faith in Christ. We also came to the realization that practically all of the remaining areas of the world that have never been penetrated by the gospel are situated west and south of China. We believe God has given us a solemn responsibility to take the fire from his altar and complete the Great Commission by establishing his kingdom in all of the remaining countries and people groups in Asia, the Middle East, and Islamic North Africa. When this happens, we believe the Scripture says the Lord Jesus Christ will return for his bride and *"we who are still alive and are left will be caught up together with them in the clouds to meet the Lord in the air. And so we will be with the Lord forever. Therefore encourage each other with these words"* (1 Thess. 4:17–18).

We believe that the farthest the gospel can travel from Jerusalem is to circle the entire globe and come all the way back to where it started—Jerusalem! When the fire of the gospel completes its circuit of the whole globe, the Lord Jesus will return! *"For the earth will be filled with the knowledge of the glory of the Lord, as the waters cover the sea"* (Hab. 2:14). This is where the name "Back to Jerusalem" comes from in terms of the missionary vision of the church in China.

Having shared some of the biblical basis for the Back to Jerusalem movement, and some of our understanding about how the gospel has spread around the world throughout history, it is time to move on to describe some of the early efforts of pioneer Back to Jerusalem missionaries in the 1940s.

# 3

# The Back to Jerusalem Evangelistic Band

*The Lord will lay bare his holy arm in the sight of all the nations, and all the ends of the earth will see the salvation of our God.*

*— Isaiah 52:10*

In the early 1940s, God gave a clear call to a small group of Christians studying at the Northwest Bible Institute in Shaanxi Province. This institute had been founded by James Hudson Taylor II (the grandson of the world-famous pioneer) and his wife Alice when bombing during the Japanese invasion of China forced them to leave Henan Province. They traveled westward into Shaanxi Province, where they had the vision to establish a Bible school. Prayer for land for the school was answered when the China Inland Mission offered them premises near the city of Fengxiang. It was a beautiful facility surrounded by a thick bamboo grove, with leafy trees ringing the single-storied buildings of the classrooms, student dormitories, and missionaries' homes.

It was in these beautiful surroundings that God gave a clear call to a small group of Christians, led by Pastor Mark Ma, the vice-principal of the Institute. God challenged them to move beyond their evangelistic outreach to Muslims, Buddhists, and scattered Chinese living in Gansu, Qinghai, and Ningxia provinces and to consecrate themselves to the vision of carrying the gospel outside China's borders into the Islamic world, all the way back to Jerusalem.

## Mark Ma and the Founding of the Back to Jerusalem Band

Mark Ma was a native of Henan Province. The only son of Christian parents, he was educated in the ancient city of Kaifeng and became

23

a teacher in a government school. However, he refused to open his heart to the Lord until 1937, when the tragic death of his little son broke his heart and brought him in sorrow and repentance to the foot of the cross. He left his secular job and went into training at the Free Methodist Bible School. When Mr. and Mrs. James Taylor fled to Shaanxi, Mark Ma, his wife, and their several children accompanied them. He became a founding staff member of the Northwest Bible Institute.

Early in 1942, Mark Ma had a discussion with the Lord that changed his life forever and gave him the momentum needed for pioneer work into the vast unreached Muslim world. We have his own account of what happened then, and in the months that followed:[18]

> On the evening of November 25, 1942, while in prayer the Lord said to me, "The door to Xinjiang is already open. Enter and preach the gospel." When this voice reached me I was trembling and fearful and most unwilling to obey, because I did not recall a single time in the past when I had prayed for Xinjiang; moreover it was a place which I had no desire to go. Therefore I merely prayed about this matter, not even telling my wife.

Xinjiang, meaning "New Dominion," is a vast region of northwest China that has traditionally been known as Eastern Turkestan. It was, and still is, inhabited by millions of Muslims, the majority of whom speak languages from the Turkic linguistic family, such as Uygur, Kazak, Kirgiz, and Uzbek. Other Muslim groups include Tajiks, Tatars, and Chinese-speaking Hui people. A large number of nomadic Tibetan Buddhists also inhabit Xinjiang. It is not surprising that Pastor Ma had no particular desire to go to a region of which he knew very little. His account continues:

> After exactly five months of prayer, on Easter morning, 25 April, 1943, when two fellow workers and I were praying together on the bank of the Wei River, I told them of my call to Xinjiang and one of the fellow workers said that ten years before she had received a similar call. I thanked God that He had already prepared a co-worker. When I returned to the school I learned that on that same Easter Sunday at the sunrise service eight students had also been burdened for Xinjiang.

The Easter morning service in 1943 to which he refers was to prove the genesis for a chain of events that drastically changed the lives of many. The impact of that prayer time is still felt in the Chinese church to this day. While Pastor Ma was not at the service, we have an account of the events from another source:

> On the hard surface of the courtyard, under the tall trees whose thick boughs spread a leafy shelter overhead, a map of China had been outlined in whitewash. The students stood around, looking at it. They had been hearing again of the needs of the great provinces to the North and to the West. . . . The sky was lightening in the east, and thin rays of light obliterated the fading grayness of the night. It was very silent in the courtyard, and the white-washed outline of the map on the ground stood out sharply. The solemn moment had arrived, the moment which brought with it an almost breathtaking hush. "Let those who have received the Lord's commission leave their places and go and stand on the province to which God has called them." . . . There was a stir among the group of students. Cloth-soled feet moved noiselessly as one, then another, walked across the courtyard to the map. And as the sun rose over the distant horizon, eight young people were seen standing quietly on the patch that was marked with the word XINJIANG.[19]

These were the students who joined Mark Ma in his call. His own account continues, with a vivid account of his conversation with God:

> It was with joy that I gathered them all together, and we planned to have a regular prayer meeting. With permission of the faculty we decided on Tuesday evening as the time for our weekly prayer meeting. On the evening of May 4 we held our first prayer meeting and there were 23 present. . . . On May 11 we received the first offering for our mission, amounting to $50.
>
> Gradually the question arose as to what our group should be called. . . . On the morning of May 23 as I fasted and prayed about the name of the Band the Lord revealed the verse of Scripture to my heart, *"This gospel of the kingdom shall be preached in all the world, for a witness unto all nations; and then the end shall come"* (Matt. 24:14).
>
> I said, "O Lord what does this mean?" The Lord replied, "It is this, I not only want the Chinese church to assume responsibility for taking the gospel to Xinjiang but I want you to bring to completion the commission to preach the gospel to all the world." I asked, "O Lord, has not the gospel already been preached to all the world?"
>
> The Lord said, "Since the beginning at Pentecost, the Pathway of the

gospel has spread, for the greater part, in a westward direction; from Jerusalem to Antioch to all Europe; from Europe to America and then to the East; from the Southeast of China to the Northwest; until today from Gansu on Westward it can be said there is no firmly established church. You may go Westward from Gansu, preaching the gospel all the way back to Jerusalem, causing the light of the gospel to complete the circle around this dark world." I said, "O Lord, who are we that we can carry such a great responsibility?" The Lord answered, "I want to manifest My power through those who of themselves have no power."

I said, "That section of territory is under the power of Islam and the Muslims are the hardest of all peoples to reach with the gospel."

The Lord replied, "The most rebellious people are the Israelites, the hardest field of labor is my own people the Jews." . . . The Lord continued speaking, "Even you Chinese, yourself included, are hard enough but you have been conquered by the gospel."

I asked, "O Lord, if it is not that their hearts are especially hard, why is it that missionaries from Europe and America have established so many churches in China but are still unable to open the door to Western Asia?"

The Lord answered me, "It is not that their hearts are especially hard, but I have kept for the Chinese church a portion of inheritance, otherwise, when I return will you not be so poor?"

When I heard the Lord say He had kept for us a portion of inheritance, my heart overflowed with Thanksgiving and my mouth uttered many Hallelujahs! I stopped arguing with the Lord.

On May 23, 1943, Mark Ma reported the above revelation to the prayer group. They decided they needed a name for their group and settled on Bian Chuan Fuyin Tuan, which literally means the "Preach Everywhere Gospel Band." This is the name this small group of faith-filled men and women are known by in China to this day, but the missionaries agreed that the English name of the movement should be the "Back to Jerusalem Evangelistic Band."

One of the missionaries who played a key role in the early days of this band was Helen Bailey, an American Presbyterian missionary who had lived in China for quarter of a century. She lived on the premises of the Northwest Bible Institute and was deeply loved by the students and faculty. She nurtured and encouraged the vision God had given to the young Chinese men and women, but when they invited her to join the Band She wisely declined, believing it was primarily a call to the Chinese church and should therefore remain an indigenous movement.

It was the policy of the leaders of the Band not to solicit finances in any way, but to pray and trust God to provide for all their needs. Donations started coming in from all over China from believers whose hearts were touched by the vision and who were moved to participate. Helen Taylor commented:

> In a remarkable way money came into the treasury almost entirely from Chinese sources and they felt that they must use up what was sent in and trust God to send more. Chinese Christians from many places, hearing of this work sent generous offerings. It was manifest that the movement was God-inspired.[20]

Despite the urgency of the call, it was not until 1944 that three women and two men were sent to Lanzhou in Gansu Province for a short term of service. In 1945 two men were sent to preach the gospel among the Hui Muslims in Ningxia. In 1946 the Lord called two men, Mecca Chao and Timothy Tai, to go northwest into Xinjiang for a longer term of service.

Now that the call was being acted on in a more serious manner, a business meeting was held on May 15, 1946 at which a constitution was accepted and officers elected, thus formerly organizing the Back to Jerusalem Evangelistic Band. The constitution included the following statements:

> This is an inter-denominational but not an anti-denominational group of workers accepting the whole Bible as God's revelation. Its aim is to join members of the Lord's body in fellowship to consecrate strength and will on the preaching of the gospel in order to be ready for the Lord's return. The sphere of the work is two-fold:

> First, pioneer work is as follows:

> 1) In the seven provinces on the borders of China: Xinjiang, Inner Mongolia, Tibet, Xikang [Tibetan areas of today's western Sichuan], Qinghai, Gansu, Ningxia.

> 2) In the seven countries on the borders of Asia: Afghanistan, Iran, Arabia, Iraq, Syria, Turkey and Palestine.

> Second, concerning the establishment of new churches in evangelized areas as well as the shepherding and reviving of existing churches, in pioneer districts we plan to establish churches according to the

example of Scripture. In places where churches already exist, we plan to serve such churches. We look to the Lord alone for all financial supplies.[21]

Mark Ma was always considered the leader of the Back to Jerusalem Evangelistic Band. In addition to his responsibilities as vice-principal of the Northwest Bible Institute and his busy schedule of evangelistic work, he assumed the added responsibility of traveling throughout China, "calling the church to prayer and spiritual warfare on behalf of the Back to Jerusalem Evangelistic Band, and enlisting volunteers for service in this great work."[22]

The following words of Mark Ma ring true for the present generation of Chinese believers who are now pressing forward with consecrated hearts to fulfil this great call:

> My hope is that our Chinese church will with determination and courage hold fast this great responsibility and, depending upon our all victorious Saviour, complete this mighty task, and taking possession of our glorious inheritance, take the gospel back to Jerusalem. There we shall stand on the top of Mount Zion and welcome our Lord Jesus Christ descending with clouds in great glory!

# The Pioneers

In March 1947 two men and five women set out on the long westward trek to Xinjiang. Each carried only one small bag and a washbasin. (The washbasins can be seen in the photograph taken before they set out.) In a magazine of the Back to Jerusalem Band that appeared before the team's departure, they wrote:

> THE TIME FOR WORK HAS ARRIVED!
>
> OPEN FAITH WARFARE!
>
> These are God's words to us. He has indicated that some are soon to leave for the Northwest. So we see it is not only His message to us, but it is a command—an urgent command to advance. It is a message that involves the sword and blood, but also the crown and song. Because of this it frightens the weak, but makes the blood of the strong to mount up.
>
> Praise the Lord, there are already five women of Fengxiang called of the Lord, and following His commission, who have decided to leave for the West next March (1947). Perhaps the prophecy of Psalm 68:11 (R.V.)

will soon be fulfilled in our midst, *"The Lord gave the word; great was the company of women who published it."* Realizing the dangers and hardships of the road ahead of them, we fear it is not one which young women should ordinarily travel, but one of them has said, "We may not reach there, we may die on the way, but we are willing to shed our blood on the highway to Mount Zion." . . . This shows the caliber of our young women missionaries. But what about the men? Brethren, awake![23]

Who were these women? Their names were Ho En Cheng, Lu Teh, Li Chin Chuan, Fan Chi Chieh, and Wei Suxi. We know something about their stories and about how they came to be embarking on such a dangerous journey, and will focus briefly on three of them.

*Ho En Cheng (Grace Ho)* had been dedicated to God by her mother when she was a newborn baby. As a little girl she was well acquainted with Bible stories and pasted the names of places such as Jerusalem, Bethany, and Mount Zion around the family courtyard! After graduating from Bible School in Tianjin in 1937, the seventeen-year-old Ho En Cheng received a clear call from the Lord to take the gospel into Xinjiang, and ultimately all the way back to Jerusalem:

> She was attending an evangelistic meeting, and as the congregation rose to pray, she received a vision from the Lord. Her immediate surroundings faded from her vision, and she seemed to be standing alone in a vast, bright wilderness plain. In the distance she heard a voice—a voice full of sorrow, painfully crying for help. She looked but saw no one, only the horror of great darkness, from whence the sound of great anguish came. Then, as she gazed, another voice spoke, a Voice from heaven, deep with mercy and compassion. "The people in the darkness have no one to preach the Good News to them." Greatly moved at the sound of that Voice, the tears springing to her eyes, she replied, "O Lord, here am I."[24]

Ten years later, after becoming part of the Back to Jerusalem Evangelistic Band, Ho's plan was to travel to the city of Kashgar—the western most point in China—to study the Turkic and Arabic languages before leaving China for Central Asia and the Middle East.

*Lu Teh (Ruth Lu)* hailed from Fengqiu County in Henan Province. She was saved by the Lord in 1940 and developed a great passion for lost souls. She ended up attending the Northwest Bible Institute. She remembers:

One day as I knelt in prayer the Lord called me by name and in a vision showed me the desolate, pitiful spiritual condition of the Northwest. I saw a multitude of lost souls in a mountain valley crying for help to save their lives. Having gone astray, they did not know how to find the True God who could save them. The voice of God said to me, "My child, are you willing to go and save them?" When this voice pierced my heart, without hesitation I replied, "O Lord, your handmaiden is willing to obey Your will."[25]

This young woman's call was to travel to Kashgar in Xinjiang to learn languages that would help her reach into Afghanistan.

*Li Chin Chuan* was born into a Muslim home. Her parents died while she was still very young, and she went to live with her grandmother. When just twelve years old, she ran away from home and fell into a life of sin. At the age of twenty she heard the gospel of Jesus Christ for the first time. She believed in the Lord and was saved. In 1941 she entered the Northwest Bible Institute. Three years later, in 1944, Li was one of those who went on a short-term outreach to Lanzhou in Gansu Province where she met Tibetan people. After returning to the Bible school, Li Chin Chuan found that:

the Lord suddenly touched my heart to see the pitiful need of the Tibetan people. At that time I did not have the courage to respond to God's call, but after returning from Lanzhou the appeal constantly presented itself before me, and I could not but accept this challenge from God. . . . The Lord put the load of Tibet on my heart—planted it deep down in my heart.[26]

In March 1947 she joined the other Back to Jerusalem missionaries and headed westward.

The two men in this pioneer group of missionaries were Chang Moxie (Moses Chang) and Mecca Chao. As Mecca Chao was the one who left the most detailed record, we will concentrate on telling his story.

*Mecca Chao* was born in Linxian, Henan Province, in east-central China. When he was a child his family fled to Shanxi Province to escape famine. In his late teens Chao entered into a relationship with Jesus Christ and his life changed forever. His heart had been so deeply touched by the love of God that he unreservedly dedicated himself to the King of Kings, promising to go wherever he should lead him, to do whatever his master required of him.

A short time after he had been saved, Mecca Chao was praying for God's guidance concerning his pathway in life when he received a vision in which he saw a piece of paper being held before his eyes with the word "Mecca" written upon it. He had no idea what this word meant and eagerly asked his fellow Christians if they knew, but nobody could help him. Mecca Chao testified, "Now I know that Jesus is the true God, the living God; I have heard His voice and He has shown me clearly the way wherein I should go."[27]

In his first year as a believer, Mecca Chao experienced God in a similar way to countless Chinese house church Christians today. His life was characterized by deep repentance and zeal coupled with intense spiritual warfare.

> At this time my zeal was very fervent. . . . God gave me a special power in prayer. At each service we only read the Bible, sang and prayed. Every time I prayed the Holy Spirit worked, convicting the hearts of the people so that they wept and confessed their sins. . . . This continued for half a year but the devil was working in great power – assaulting me on every side; especially when I prayed he manifested his wicked power. He often brought before me fearful, strange-looking beings to frighten me, causing me to pray less and less, until finally I did not dare to pray at all. . . . Gradually I fell into temptation. My spiritual life grew colder and colder each day. . . . I walked the way of the world, the ambition for position and gain taking the place of God in my life. . . . The heavenly Father's loving heart must have been sorely wounded, but in my disobedience I did not realize how His heart was grieved.[28]

For the next several years the backslidden Mecca Chao fought in the Chinese army, facing death every day and feeling miserable within. He was captured during battle and became a prisoner of war, experiencing dreadful torture and deprivation. It was while behind bars that the Lord lovingly called his prodigal son back to his embrace. In his dingy, isolated prison cell the Lord started to revive Mecca Chao's spirit and remind him of everything he had walked away from. "I asked the Lord, 'O God, is this the kind of life that "Mecca" means? Is this the way wherein I should go?'"

The Lord responded by giving him a vision of a map of Ningxia Province, the seat of Islam in China. In another vision he saw a long bright road leading westward along which he must one day travel. He later said,

God was thinking of me and gave me a ray of hope to dispel a little of my prison despondency. He promised me that at the age of twenty-five I would leave the prison and at the age of twenty-seven I would take up the work committed to me. It happened exactly in this way. In May of my twenty-fifth year I was delivered from prison and in July of my twenty-sixth year I came to the Northwest Bible Institute as a student. In my twenty-seventh year I went on preaching tours to Gansu Province and in the summer to the place I had seen in the vision – Ningxia Province. We must truly rely on the faithfulness of God.[29]

Chao's zeal had now been balanced with substance, and he hungered to know God's word in an intimate and knowledgeable way. He testified:

After passing through seven or eight years of sore testing, often times in extreme difficulty and danger, I had come through at last to a state of peace and calm. Had it not been for my Heavenly Father's great power, which was my sole protection, I should long ago have returned to dust. Although I had become greatly weakened because of the hardships of the past several years, even so I was much stronger than when I had left home years before, a thin, yellow, weakly specimen of humanity. Hallelujah! This was God's wonderful protection over His child in order that He might use him in the Northwest. Yes, Lord, I am willing for You to use me as You please. You are the potter, I am the clay. . . . The Lord understands me perfectly, I belong to Him. I am bought with a price, never again should I make my own plans. . . . He merely asks that I leave myself utterly in His hands to be used by Him.[30]

While studying at the Northwest Bible Institute Mecca Chao had the mystery of the word "Mecca" solved for him by Mark Ma. Ma told him the commission he had received several years before was to travel westward to preach the gospel to the Muslims, going on until he reached the city of Mecca in Saudi Arabia.

When Mecca Chao learned about the vision God had given the leaders of the school to take the gospel back to Jerusalem, he was amazed to find it exactly matched his own call. Not surprisingly, he enthusiastically enlisted in the mission and became one of the first workers of the Back to Jerusalem Evangelistic Band.

As Mecca Chao and the other six pioneers prepared to set out, Christians all around China were excited at their pending departure. Many prayers went up for the success of the venture and the protection of those involved. Bishop F. Houghton summarized the impact of the faith of these young pioneers:

> The church in China has been stirred through the going forth of a group of Chinese workers from the Northwest Bible Institute. From a preliminary base at Xining they are planning to go forward into Xinjiang, and thence—eventually—to carry the gospel through Central Asia 'back to Jerusalem!' They show the marks of a Divine call in their fervent abandon to His will and equally in a sensible, practical attitude which reminds one of Hudson Taylor.[31]

These seven faith-filled pioneers traveled three hundred miles northwest to Xining, now the capital city of Qinghai Province. There they were met by Pastor Su, who encouraged them to consider the spiritual needs of Xining City and to stay and study Arabic for a while. The team felt that this offer did not represent God's will for them, and their desire to keep moving westward towards Xinjiang was undiminished. After a day's journey they arrived at Huangyuan. From there Mecca Chao continued alone to Tulan (now called Ulan) in Qinghai Province, a distance of 265 miles (429 km), to prepare the way for the rest of the team to follow. Tulan was considered the last outpost of Chinese civilization. It was also a communication hub through which caravans from Central Asia traveled, and so was a strategic location for the team to start learning some of the languages spoken by Central Asian Muslims.

Mecca Chao traveled these miles on horseback. He suffered terribly from neuralgia, and reported that at one town where he stopped he was "very miserable, and only able to go to the school and a medicine shop and talk about the gospel a little with the teacher and the shopkeeper."[32]

The difficulties of this journey through areas infested by bandits can be seen from his letter to Mark Ma. After announcing his arrival, Mecca Chao wrote, "First let me say a most important word – on no account let anyone come this road without very clear and definite guidance from the Lord." Some of the reasons for this statement can be found in his descriptions of his journey:

> Only to think of the difficulties and dangers of this road is enough to make your hair stand on end. All along the way are the pasture grounds of the wild Tibetans, Mongols and Muslims, who live in tents. There are no inns. There are high mountains of grassy deserts,

packs of wild animals, man-eating Tibetan dogs, and murderous
bandits. ...

Along the road there were many bodies of those who had been
starved to death or killed. ... Every night I looked carefully to see
there was no one in sight, and then quietly went into the thick grass
hidden from the road. There I took the pack off the horse, and slept
under the open sky. I didn't dare make a sound for fear of attracting
robbers. Sometimes along the road I heard firing, but I was quite at
rest, and in fact I did not encounter any danger. Travelers all carry
guns; my gun was prayer. ... God let me prove the strength of a
Hallelujah to scare away robbers and wild beasts, and meet every
difficulty.[33]

Some months later the rest of the Back to Jerusalem team advanced
westward to join Mecca Chao in Tulan. It was agreed that:

some of the party should set up a home at Tulan which should be the
last connecting link between the Chinese home church and the new
mission fields. They also decided that a small group of workers should
proceed first and break the way for others who were to follow, for too
large a party would arouse suspicion from the areas through which
they would pass. While they were awaiting government permission
and travel documents they busied themselves making inquires about
caravan routes, the most economical modes of travel and the customs
of the peoples who they should encounter, but at the same time they
divided up into evangelistic groups and went out preaching.[34]

Finding that camel travel was much less expensive and far less
dangerous than bus travel, they decided to purchase camels. The
locals found the sight of Chinese preachers trying to buy camels
humorous, and the Band was delayed for two weeks while they
negotiated for a fair price with local Muslims.

In late July 1947, they set out again on their long journey westward,
anxious to reach their destination before the short summer months
in this part of the world ended and winter snowfall made progress
impossible. The first stage of ninety miles across swampy marshes
and high mountains took them six days. When they finally reached
the border with Xinjiang, they were detained for several days while
their passports were certified by the border officials. Permission was
finally granted, and the small band of gospel warriors crossed "into
the lion's mouth."

The vision God had given Mark Ma, Mecca Chao, and the others was finally being fulfilled, and Chinese missionaries were making their way into the Islamic world with the fire of the gospel burning in their hearts.

For the next month they travelled through desert wastes, with few signs of human existence except a small village here and there. Drinking water was scarce. Wherever they could, they filled their containers, but many days would pass between opportunities to refill. Hundreds of travelers had perished in this region, their throats cut and their goods plundered by ruthless bandits. It is no wonder that the desert is known as the Taklimakan—a word from the Uygur language that can be loosely translated as "Many go in but few come out." Yet the missionaries continued onward, aware of God's protection at all times.

And then disaster struck.

# A Vision Delayed

One month into their desert journey, the Back to Jerusalem Band's camel train was met by government officials who informed them that permission to travel further had been withdrawn due to new political developments in the region. They were told to return to China proper. Despite their prayers and pleadings, the officials rejected their every request, saying it was unsafe and foolish for such a collection of youngsters, mostly women, to travel through the Taklimakan Desert. "Since no amount of persuasion on their part could convince the officials that theirs was not a political mission and that they were not afraid of the dangers en route, it was necessary for them to retrace their steps back to Qinghai."[35]

After much prayer they decided to wait out the winter in Qinghai, busy about their Master's business, after which they would attempt to enter Xinjiang again by another route. They continued their evangelistic work, seeing many people won to the Lord.

It was while they were waiting for the door to Xinjiang to open that the Communists swept to power in China. Soon after a curtain of silence descended across the nation. All foreign missionaries were expelled from the country and communication came to a halt. In the face of a systematic plan to obliterate the church, believers such as Mark Ma, Mecca Chao and Ho En Cheng went "underground." As the months of persecution and hardship rolled into years, and years into decades, the vision of the Back to Jerusalem Band began to fade. All seemed lost. Like the children of Israel who were so close to the Promised Land that they could see it with their eyes, the Back to Jerusalem vision in the late 1940s and early 1950s was taken back into the wilderness, to await a time when the workers would be better equipped to handle the great task laid before them.

# A Vision Rekindled

Helen Taylor, whose family had been instrumental in training and encouraging the Back to Jerusalem workers at the Northwest Bible Institute, wrote the following prayer request after the Band had been sent back to Qinghai in 1948:

> Will you help these young people with your prayers? The powers of evil in these darkened corners of the earth which are the habitation of cruelty and violence will not easily yield to the light of the gospel, but through prayer we may see the walls of brass tottering before these Spirit-filled young people who are going forth under the banner of Him who never lost a battle. Who will uphold them in prayer?[36]

This prayer request is being repeated thousands of times throughout China today, as a new generation of better-prepared Christians follow in the footsteps and fulfil the vision of the original Back to Jerusalem Evangelistic Band.

Could it be that God allowed the original Back to Jerusalem efforts to be thwarted because the Chinese church was not yet ready to succeed in this great call? When the vision first sprang up, the Protestant church in China numbered less than a million and the Back to Jerusalem vision was taken up by a very small number of individuals. Miraculously, more than fifty years later the Chinese church numbers approximately 80 to 100 million members and countless thousands of believers are responding to the Back to Jerusalem call. *"For the revelation awaits an appointed time; it speaks of the end and will not prove false. Though it linger, wait for it; it will certainly come and will not delay"* (Hab. 2:3).

To the human eye, the Back to Jerusalem Evangelistic Band failed. But God knew the dedication of his young children, and did not

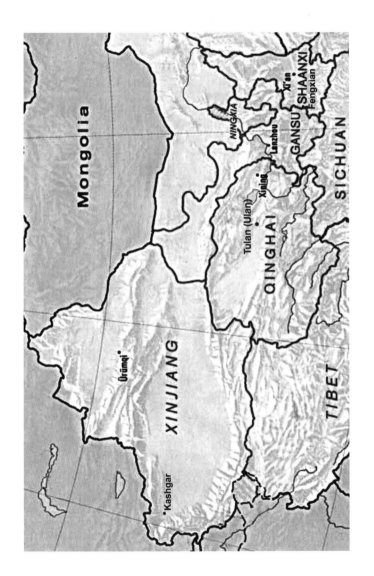

Map 3. A map of Northwest China that shows the principal staging posts of the Back to Jerusalem Evangelistic Band in the 1940s.

reject the purity of their commitment to him. Although the vision was buried for a time, it did not perish.

Nor did all the members of the original band. A few of them are still alive, having survived more than half a century of affliction in the fire of persecution. Ho En Cheng, now in her eighties, still lives in the heart of Xinjiang where she reaches out to Muslims and continues to share the Back to Jerusalem vision with any Christian who will stop to listen.

God has, as always, been faithful to his children.

# 4

# The Northwest Spiritual Movement

*I tell you the truth, unless a kernel of wheat falls to the ground and dies, it remains only a single seed. But if it dies, it produces many seeds. The man who loves his life will lose it, while the man who hates his life in this world will keep it for eternal life.*

*— John 12:24–25*

The Back to Jerusalem Band who met at the Northwest Bible Institute in Shaanxi Province were not the only Chinese believers whom God was calling to minister to the Muslim peoples to the west. Nor were they even the first. That honor seems to belong to a group called the Jesus Family who formed in the 1920s.

The Jesus Family was founded in 1921 in Shandong Province by a man named Jing Dianying. Its members believed that they should sell all their possessions and distribute their wealth among the other family members. The group's five-word slogan encapsulated their commitment to Christ and their pattern of frugal living: "Sacrifice, abandonment, poverty, suffering, death."

The Jesus Family targeted towns and villages, preaching the gospel as they walked from one place to another. Their example of communal living and their deep Christian love amazed many onlookers. It attracted those searching for answers to life as well as those who were homeless, destitute, and despised. Many blind people and beggars joined the Jesus Family and found eternal life in Christ.

As they continued to grow, the Jesus Family suffered terrible hardships. Often when this mobile community entered a new town the entire population would come out to beat, scorn, and humiliate them. The opposition didn't deter them, however, and when they preached the gospel there always seemed to be a few people willing to forsake all that they had to follow Jesus.

The Jesus Family was the first to have the Back to Jerusalem vision. Their workers carried baskets of food and essentials as they walked on foot across China. By the late 1940s there were some twenty thousand Chinese believers enlisted in more than one hundred different Jesus Family groups throughout China, enabling them to reach many different regions with the gospel. Some believers went to Manchuria, some to Inner Mongolia, others to southern China. All of these groups considered themselves part of the Back to Jerusalem vision. They all prayerfully and practically supported the main evangelistic band that was heading west into the Muslim nations on foot, intending to establish the kingdom of God in all the territories along the way.

Yet it seems that after a time the Jesus Family lost their direction. All the authority was invested in the one leader, Jing Dianying. Consequently the Back to Jerusalem vision became extremely centralized and was not shared by most of the ordinary believers. A split developed and a new group, known as the Northwest Spiritual Movement emerged. Today's Chinese believers interpret this split in different ways. Some say that it was a bad thing, while others believe the Lord was behind it because the vision was floundering and a fresh start had to be made.

Whatever the case, by the end of the 1930s God had raised up a new generation of believers who were willing to forsake everything in obedience to seeing this call of God completed. They said, "Let's rise to our feet and carry the cross to the nations where God is not known. Let's go forth in Jesus' name, giving up everything we have, even our very lives if necessary, so that the name of Jesus will be glorified among all the Gentiles." Most of the original leaders of this group hailed from Shandong Province, including the founder, Zhang Guquan.

The strategy of the Northwest Spiritual Movement was simply to preach the gospel, believing that Jesus would soon return. They did not spend any effort on establishing local congregations, concentrating solely on evangelism and soul winning. Yet God in his mercy still established many new believers and there was much fruit that remains to this day. They won people to Christ among many ethnic groups including Muslim Uygurs, Hui, and Kazaks.

You need to understand that this was not a large spiritual army marching across the nation. The leadership consisted of just four or five individuals, plus a few dozen other workers. But despite their small numbers the Northwest Spiritual Movement was effective because their vision was focused. They were like a sharp arrowhead, while the new converts they left behind were the shaft of the arrow.

In addition to the Back to Jerusalem Evangelistic Band and the Northwest Spiritual Movement, there were several smaller initiatives by different Chinese church groups in the 1940s. Some reached into Tibetan areas, others to the minorities of southwest China, still others into the Muslim regions. Yet despite their different origins and spheres of work, all of these groups considered themselves part of the larger vision to carry the gospel back to Jerusalem.

Writing in 1949, Phyllis Thompson, a worker based in Chongqing with the China Inland Mission, remarked:

> The thing that has impressed me most has been the strange, unaccountable urge of a number of different Chinese groups of Christians to press forward in faith, taking the gospel towards the west. I know of at least five different groups, quite unconnected with each other, who have left their homes in east China and gone forth, leaving practically everything behind them, to the west. Some are in Xikang [now western Sichuan], some in Gansu, some right away in the great northwestern province of Xinjiang. It seems like a movement of the Spirit which is irresistible. The striking thing is that they are disconnected, and in most cases seem to know nothing about each other. Yet all are convinced that the Lord is sending them to the western borders to preach the gospel, and they are going with a strong sense of urgency of the shortness of the time, and the imminence of the Lord's return.[37]

# Simon Zhao

We will tell the story of one man who while still in his early thirties was appointed the leader of preaching and evangelism in the Northwest Spiritual Movement.

Born on June 1, 1918, Simon Zhao (whose original name was Zhao Haizhen) was originally from Shenyang in Liaoning Province in northeast China. His father died when Simon was a young boy, and his mother was forced to raise the children alone. She was a beautiful woman. On several occasions the village leader came to their home and tried to lure her to commit adultery with him. He brought her expensive gifts but grew more and more frustrated as she repulsed his advances. Finally, tired of her resistance, he raped her.

When little Simon found out what had happened to his beloved mother he was furious. He told his mother that when he grew up he would become a county leader so that he could bring the man to justice for the wrongs done to her. His mother replied, "It's no use. The county leaders are just as corrupt as that evil village leader."

"Then I will become higher than the county leaders!" Simon exclaimed.

"It's no use. The provincial leaders are just as corrupt as the county leaders," his mother replied.

"Then I will be a higher leader than the provincial leaders!"

"Again, son, it's no use. The emperor is just the same."

Simon was heartbroken and angry and asked his mother, "Then who is more powerful than the emperor? Where can we go for justice?"

His mother replied, "Only God can grant justice, my son."

"Then I will become a god!" the zealous little boy concluded.

The wound in Simon's heart did not mend. In his teens he pursued a career as a writer and used his skills to expose the village leader's crimes in a local newspaper. Yet his anger still burned.

Many years later, Simon Zhao met God. He found that he no longer hated and sought revenge on the man who had violated his mother. His goals in life had changed, and now all he wanted to do was preach the gospel and make the glory of God known.

It was during a prayer meeting in Shenyang that the Lord first gave Simon a vision. It was winter and very cold. Outside the house where the believers prayed, the snowdrifts grew so high that the doors were blocked and they could not leave. As three believers were praying over a map of China, the Lord focused their thoughts on the northwest province of Xinjiang. They placed their hands over that part of China on the map and prayed with great authority. Before that day they had never seriously considered ministry in the remote northwest.

Later, in Nanjing, Simon met other Christians who had received exactly the same vision from God to take the gospel to Xinjiang and the regions beyond. Among them was a young woman named Wen

Muling, who later became his wife. She was a fourth generation descendent of a Qing dynasty imperial officer.

Three teams set out to join in the harvest. The first group reached Xinjiang, and was followed by Simon Zhao's group. Later a third group, under the leadership of Zhu Congen from Zibo in Shandong Province, made their way on foot into Xinjiang after the advent of Communism in China in 1949.

The group led by Simon Zhao and his wife left Nanjing and traveled to Xinjiang via Shaanxi Province. For much of the way they went on foot, but there were some areas such as the desert where it was impossible to walk, and so they also traveled on horseback, camelback, and occasionally by vehicle, all the time heading for the northwest border with the Soviet Union. On the way they won many soldiers to faith in Christ, for it was a troubled time in China's history with civil war and widespread internal chaos.

Eventually they reached Hami on the eastern edge of Xinjiang and joined members of the North West [Spiritual Movement] who had arrived there a year or two previously. Eager to plant the gospel on virgin soil, Zhao headed south with five fellow workers to Hetian, a remote oasis town in the far south of Xinjiang, in the winter of 1950. But two weeks after they arrived the Public Security Bureau ordered them to leave. So they were forced to move even further west to Kashgar, where in September 1949 the Band had set up a preaching station at Shule....They arrived in January 1950 to a chaotic situation. The gospel compound had been taken over by armed soldiers who claimed there had been a 'counter-revolutionary incident.' Uncle Simon did not know what to make of it. But within a few days he was arrested and placed in prison.[38]

Every member of the Northwest Spiritual Movement was sentenced to prison, for various lengths of time. The five leaders were given extremely harsh sentences—Simon Zhao was the only one to see out his sentence alive. His wife was pregnant at the time of their arrest, but soon after she suffered a miscarriage. In 1959 she died in the women's prison, but cruelly, Simon wasn't told about it until 1973.

During the first few weeks and months in the Kashgar prison labor camp, the guards tried to make Simon renounce his faith, but they soon learned this would not work. They ordered him to stop praying and beat him every time they found him doing so. He never stopped praying, but learned to do so in secret when nobody was watching.

After some time the prison authorities thought he must have changed because they never saw him praying, so they ordered the former writer to pen a column for the prison newspaper, praising the transforming power of the Communist system.

He commenced work on the article, which greatly pleased the prison authorities. When they saw what he had written, however, they flew into a rage and realized they had been tricked. His article consisted of a short poem about the beauty of Jesus and a sketch of the cross.

The prison guards beat him by slamming a heavy wooden bench on his back and kicked him mercilessly. The local authorities punished him by extending his prison sentence for many more years and sending him to work in a coal mine, where most prisoners died within six months because of the inhuman conditions and backbreaking work. Every day he was required to meet a quota of several tons of coal, a task humanly impossible for such a small and frail man. Not only did he have to mine the coal, he also had to carry it out of the mine in a basket tied to his back.

The prisoners were forced to work fourteen hours a day, seven days a week. The food was meager and rancid. In the summer, there was sweltering heat; in the harsh winter, temperatures were well below freezing. Simon Zhao became a living miracle of God's sustaining power. Hundreds of fellow prisoners came to the coal mine, most of them physically stronger than Simon, only to die within a few months of their arrival.

For years Simon discreetly witnessed to many of his fellow prisoners, and some believed. There were a few other Christian pastors in the labor camp with him, but the authorities placed them in separate cells and work units, allowing Simon only fleeting moments of contact with them. For all the years he remained in confinement, Simon was not allowed to receive any visitors. He knew in his heart that nobody remembered him anyway in this remote Muslim border town, thousands of miles from his home.

Except for the faithful presence of his Lord, who had promised never to leave him or forsake him, Simon felt completely alone and abandoned. Back in his home province of Liaoning on the opposite side of the country, his relatives did not know whether he was dead or alive, and as the years of silence stretched into decades, few people thought about or prayed for him.

The Back to Jerusalem vision truly went underground. The seed had died.

Simon later recalled how, during those harsh years, he would look up at the stars and remember the vision God had given him and his co-workers to take the gospel all the way back to Jerusalem on foot. He had heard that his precious wife and unborn child were dead, but knew nothing about what had happened to his co-workers. So in the early years of his imprisonment, when the guards and his fellow prisoners weren't watching, Simon often prayed, "Lord, I will never be able to go back to Jerusalem, but I pray you will raise up a new generation of Chinese believers who will complete the vision." But over time Simon Zhao lost the fire and passion for the Back to Jerusalem vision, although he never denied the Lord Jesus who had given him that vision.

After many years of suffering in the coal mine Simon was almost dead, so the prison authorities transferred him to a chemical factory in another area of Xinjiang. Although this was a commercial factory, they used prisoners as their main source of labor.

This new job was little better than the mine, for he was daily exposed to toxic gases and poisonous chemicals. Every evening after work he returned to the prison, where the beatings continued. Now, however, most of them were at the hands of his fellow prisoners. The guards had devised a plan to get the prisoners to vent their frustrations on each other, rewarding those who reported on the behavior of others. Being a hated Christian whom the authorities had never been able to break, Simon Zhao was a particularly easy target for brutal men.

Yet God had not forgotten him. On one occasion in the midst of a severe winter, the prison guards refused to let Simon stay in the heated cell block. They stripped him to his underwear and forced him to stand outside in the snow. As they pushed him out the door they mocked him, saying, "You believe in your God, so why don't you pray to him and ask him to keep you warm!"

For the first few minutes the cold wind tore into his flesh like a razor. Simon cried out to the Lord for mercy—and something amazing happened. He felt a tremendous warmth, so much so that he soon had sweat dripping off his body as though he were relaxing in a sauna! The snow around his feet started to melt away from the warmth emanating from his body. He called out to his cell mates inside and when they looked out the window they could scarcely believe their eyes. Steam was rising from his body!

Yet such dramatic miracles were uncommon, and he suffered terribly. Hundreds of times he was beaten mercilessly. The majority of the prisoners were ethnic Uygurs, the predominant Muslim people in Xinjiang. The Uygur prisoners were especially cruel to Simon because he was a hated Chinese "pig eater". He later described the way the Uygurs beat him as "the same way they surround and pounce on a goat just before they kill it."

Once he was beaten and kicked so severely that his skull was fractured and he fell to the ground unconscious. While unconscious, he had a vision in which the Lord spoke lovingly to him, "My child, I am with you. I shall never leave you or forsake you." Regaining consciousness at that moment, he had no idea how long he had been out. He was dizzy and unsure of where he was. He touched his head on the spot where his skull had been smashed and discovered that the wound had miraculously healed, although there was dried blood on that spot.

Simon Zhao was beaten for most of the thirty-one years he spent in prison. It was only during the last several years—when he was an elderly man in his sixties—that he wasn't subjected to physical torture.

During those long years behind bars he wrote this poem:

> I want to experience the same pain and suffering
> Of Jesus on the cross
> The spear in his side, the pain in his heart
> I'd rather feel the pain of shackles on my feet
> Than ride through Egypt in Pharaoh's chariot.

One day in 1981 the prison superintendent ordered Simon to come to the main office. He walked down the corridor a little apprehensively, wondering if he had managed to get himself into more trouble. He hoped something hadn't happened that would further extend his punishment.

The superintendent invited Simon to sit down and fumbled through a thick file as he puffed on a cigarette. Finally he spoke, "The government of the People's Republic of China has decided to have mercy on you and show you lenience for the crimes you have committed against our nation. I have been authorized to release you. You are free to go."

The man of God shuffled back to his cell dazed and numb. He had never expected this day would come.

When he was first arrested in 1950, he was in the prime of his life, an energetic man in his early thirties. His beautiful young wife was expecting their first child. God had called them to take the gospel back to Jerusalem and despite the dangers and many challenges, his life was rewarding and exciting. Now, 31 years later, he was in his sixties, with white hair and a white beard.

Simon walked out the prison gates into a completely different China from the one he had known. He had missed all but the first few months of Mao Zedong's reign, including Mao's death in 1976. He had missed the insane Cultural Revolution from 1966 to 1976, when millions of people were killed by the fanatical Red Guards. He was now an old man with little strength. His body was damaged from decades of beatings, torture, and hard work, and his face was marked with deep lines revealing the struggle of more than three decades in the lion's den.

Nobody in the whole of China was waiting for him. Everyone he knew thirty-one years earlier had either died or long forgotten about him. He had nowhere to go and nobody to see. He didn't have a clue what he should do. With no money or friends, he could not even afford to catch a bus into the city.

The prison labor camp had been a part of his life for so long that he decided to construct a makeshift hut just outside the entrance to the prison. As he lay in this damp, cold hut, his mind sometimes wandered back to his life as a young man and the call God had once given him. He had faithfully tried to obey God, but it hadn't worked out. He hoped he would soon die, for he knew that heaven was a much better place and the pain and confusion he had experienced for so long would be removed forever.

For months he remained there, silent except for his daily prayers of thanksgiving to the King of Kings and Lord of Lords, who had kept his promise and never forsaken him during all those painful years. Without Jesus Christ, Simon knew he would have died a thousand deaths. The living Christ had kept him alive and sane, and had helped him to never renounce his faith in God. Simon knew that no matter how lonely a person is in this world, Jesus will always be there as *"a friend who sticks closer than a brother"* (Prov. 18:24).

After some time local Christians in Kashgar learned about Simon Zhao and heard his testimony. Out of respect they brought the old saint food and a Bible and helped him however they could.

News spread from church to church in Xinjiang about Simon, and soon the news was carried back to other parts of China that a miracle man had been sustained by the power of God during thirty-one years in prison for the sake of the gospel.

\* \* \*

Starting in the late 1960s, God poured his Spirit out on Henan Province and many millions of people experienced God's salvation there. Henan became known as the center of revival in China and was given the nickname "the Galilee of China"—the place where Jesus' disciples come from.

Many of the house church leaders in Henan had heard about the original Back to Jerusalem workers in the 1940s. Our knowledge of the details of those early workers was somewhat sketchy, but when we heard that one of the top leaders was now out of prison, we were eager to meet him and learn from him.

Some of our co-workers were ministering in Kashgar. They met Simon Zhao and sent us letters informing us of his story. Our church members in Kashgar loved him like their own father and enjoyed very close fellowship with him. He had been deprived of fellowship with other believers for decades, but now the Lord gave him spiritual sons and daughters who deeply respected him. Women from the church cooked for him, washed his clothes, and helped him however they could. They treated him as they would an angel of God.

Finally a group of house church leaders caught trains and buses all the way across China because we felt we had to meet Simon Zhao for ourselves. After more than a week of traveling, we reached Kashgar and met a broken, humble servant of God.

At that time we published a magazine which we used to encourage believers in the house churches. Simon Zhao refused to write any articles or share his testimony. We tried to show him that the current generation of Chinese believers needed to learn how the Lord had taken him through so many years of suffering. He always declined our offers, saying, "I don't want to have any attention focused on me."

Throughout the 1950s, 1960s, 1970s, and into the 1980s, there had been no active talk about taking the gospel back to Jerusalem. Times were so dark for believers in China that it took all of our energy and prayers just to survive those years with our faith intact. But in the early 1990s, the Lord showed us that it was important for Simon Zhao to come to Henan Province to share his testimony with our house church Christians in order to inspire them to carry on the vision God had given him almost fifty years before.

We sent Deborah Xu (the sister of Peter Xu, who is one of the authors of this book) by train and bus all the way to Kashgar to prayerfully persuade him to reconsider. Every day she was away we prayed that the Lord would grant her success. To start with, Simon Zhao was hesitant. He said, "The Lord called me to go west back to Jerusalem and here in Xinjiang I am at least on the way. Why should I travel back east again and go further away from Jerusalem? Why don't you leave me alone to die here in Kashgar?"

Deborah is a very persistent sister in the Lord! She wouldn't take no for an answer and followed Uncle Simon wherever he went, repeatedly asking in a loving manner if he would come back to Henan. She assured him that we had no intention of taking him away from the front line of the battle. We only wanted to bring him back to where there were thousands of new troops who needed training and equipping if the Back to Jerusalem mission was to be rekindled in the life of the Chinese church. Deborah explained that his vision could be multiplied many times over and that thousands of new recruits would be sent back to fight on the front lines if he would just come and share his story.

Finally Simon Zhao realized this sister would not give him any peace until he agreed to return to Henan Province with her. He started to realize that it must be the Lord who had given this woman such stubborn persistence! When he prayed about returning to eastern China, the Lord confirmed that he should go by giving him a Scripture that was deeply personal and brought healing after all the years of suffering and loneliness he had endured:

*"Sing, O barren woman, you who never bore a child; burst into song, shout for joy, you who were never in labor; because more are the children of the desolate woman than of her who has a husband," says the Lord. "Enlarge the place of your tent, stretch your tent curtains wide, do not hold back; lengthen your cords, strengthen your stakes. For you will spread out to the right and to the left; your descendants will dispossess nations and settle in their desolate cities. Do not be afraid; you will not suffer shame. Do not fear disgrace; you will not be humiliated. You will forget the shame of your youth and remember no more the reproach of your widowhood. For your Maker is your husband—the Lord Almighty is his name—the Holy One of Israel is your Redeemer; he is called the God of all the earth." (Isa. 54:1–5)*

We didn't have any money to buy him a sleeping berth or even a seat on the four-day train journey across China. He just found a spot on the floor and curled up on a newspaper.

When he ministered to our churches in Henan it was very powerful and a fire was lit in the heart of everyone who heard him. Many tears flowed and thousands of believers were touched and received the vision for missionary work. Even Simon Zhao's physical appearance was unique and added to his ministry. He looked like an ancient sage, with his long white beard and white hair.

For many house church leaders the Back to Jerusalem vision became very clear and God placed on us a heavy burden to see this vision fulfilled.

*       *       *

Simon Zhao finally went to be with the Lord on December 7, 2001. He was eighty-three years old. He died in Pingdingshan, Henan Province, among Christians who loved him.

His life was a remarkable one. Like Joseph, Simon started with a dream from the Lord but before it came to fulfilment he was imprisoned and his vision was put in the ground where it died while he silently suffered unjust punishment for thirty-one years, remembered by no one but God.

Yet that was not the end of the story! Unbeknown to him, the Lord was sowing this same vision in the hearts of many Christians in China. After he was finally released from prison, God graciously gave him another twenty years of ministry.

The house church Christians treated Simon Zhao with the utmost respect in the Lord and honored him as a prince in the house of God.

1. Delegates at the National Christian Conference held at Shanghai in 1907 to discuss the future of the church in China. The level of foreign control of the Chinese church at the time is clear: of the more than 800 delegates, only a handful were Chinese.

2. Some of the members of the Back to Jerusalem Evangelistic Band pictured at their farewell meeting. Left to right: Fan Chi Chieh, Lu Teh (Ruth Lu), Wei Suxi, Chang Moxie (Moses Chang), Ho En Cheng (Grace Ho), and Li Chin Chuan.

3. Thousands of Chinese Christians have suffered brutal persecution for their faith in Christ over the years. These pictures show some of the cruel methods used to restrain them in the past, including neck stocks and death cages.

4. Grace Ho and Li Chin Chuan outside their mud home at Tulan, the launch base for the Back to Jerusalem workers in 1947. Tulan is now known as Ulan township in Qinghai Province.

# The Back to Jerusalem Evangelistic Band

5. Back row: Fan Chi Chieh, Ho En Cheng (Grace Ho), Wei Suxi, Lu Teh (Ruth Lu) and Li Chin Chuan. Front row: Mecca Chao, Mark Ma, Timothy Tai.

6. Simon Zhao in 1988.

7. Brother Yun is one of the key leaders of the Back to Jerusalem movement. He is widely loved by Christians around the world and is known by his nickname "The Heavenly Man", given to him as a mark of respect by Chinese believers almost twenty years ago.

8. Peter Xu (pronounced "Shu") Yongze has been called "the Billy Graham of China". He is one of the leaders of the Back to Jerusalem movement and believes his life's work is to train workers in order to see this vision come to pass.

9. Brother Yun praying for people at the Back to Jerusalem conference in Paris, April 2003.

Before he died he came to realize that *"God's gifts and his call are irrevocable"* (Rom. 11:29).

Simon Zhao learned that the Lord always finishes what he starts and is always faithful to fulfil his promises.

# 5

# The Testimony of Brother Yun*

*Inside China Brother Yun has been imprisoned four times for the gospel, and has been arrested on more than thirty other occasions. Despite his prolonged suffering and torture, he is a man of deep joy and faith in Jesus Christ. God took Yun out of China in 1997 so that he could work to facilitate the Back to Jerusalem vision. He has spoken in more than 1,000 churches around the world since then, bringing awareness and encouraging prayer for the Chinese missionary enterprise. He is currently based in Germany with his wife, Deling, and their two children.*

When I was first saved, at the age of 16, I began to wait on the Lord for his guidance, and a wonderful thing happened. One night around 10 p.m. when I lay down on my bed, I suddenly felt someone tap my shoulder and heard a voice tell me, "Yun, I am going to send you to the west and south to be my witness."

The very next day I went to a village to the west of where I lived and shared God's word with the people there. In a way this was the start of my involvement with the Back to Jerusalem vision. Of course I had no idea at the time that most of the remaining unreached countries in the world were situated west and south of China, but as the years have passed God has slowly expanded my understanding of his original calling to me. He used Simon Zhao to be a great blessing in my life and to focus my own involvement in the Back to Jerusalem vision.

I was in prison when Simon Zhao first returned to Henan to share

---

* Most of this chapter has been paraphrased from Brother Yun's biography, *The Heavenly Man* (London: Monarch Books, 2002), chapter 24, and from recent conversations with him.

53

his experiences with the churches and so I knew nothing about him. However I had heard of the old Back to Jerusalem workers. As a relatively new Christian, I had read a booklet about their efforts to take the gospel outside China in the 1940s, only to be turned back at the last hurdle. The booklet also contained several stirring songs that the Back to Jerusalem pioneers had sung as they marched towards the west. I memorized them and taught them to others.

God was already burdening my heart and helping me understand that it was his will that the Chinese church should take the gospel into the Muslim, Buddhist and Hindu nations of the world.

In the autumn of 1995 I was speaking at a house church gathering in central China. I encouraged the believers to seek God for a worldwide vision, challenging them not only to continue in their present ministries but to expand their horizons to include the unreached nations surrounding China.

With tears in my eyes I sang one of the old songs about the Back to Jerusalem Movement:

> Lift up your eyes toward the West
> There are no laborers for the great harvest
> My Lord's heart is grieving every day
> He asks, "Who will go forth for me?"
>
> With eyes filled with tears
> And blood splattered across our chests
> We lift up the banner of Christ
> And will rescue the perishing sheep!
>
> In these last days the battle is drawing near
> And the trumpet is sounding aloud
> Let's quickly put on the full armor of God
> And break through Satan's snares!
>
> Death is knocking at the door of many
> And the world is overcome with sin
> We must faithfully work as we march onward
> Fighting even unto death!
>
> With hope and faith we will march on
> Dedicating our family and all that we have
> As we take up our heavy crosses
> We march on toward Jerusalem!

While I was singing, I noticed an old man in the congregation who was visibly moved. He was weeping and could hardly contain himself. I had no idea who he was, and thought my preaching must have been really powerful to cause such a response! The old brother, crowned with white hair and a white beard, slowly walked to the front of the room and asked to speak. A respectful hush fell over the audience. He said,

> I am Simon Zhao, a servant of the Lord. Forty-eight years ago my co-workers and I wrote the words you just sang. All of my co-workers were martyred for the name of Jesus.
>
> I was one of the leaders of the Back to Jerusalem movement. We marched across China on foot, proclaiming the gospel in every town and village we passed through. Finally in 1948, after many years of hardship, we reached the border town of Kashgar in Xinjiang Province.
>
> Before we ever had a chance to leave China, the Communist armies took control of Xinjiang. They immediately sealed the borders and implemented their strong-armed style of rule.
>
> All the leaders of our movement were arrested.... All the other leaders died in prison long ago. I am the only one who survived.... For the sake of the vision to take the gospel back to Jerusalem, I spent thirty-one years in prison for the Lord.

We were all stunned. We sat there with our mouths wide open and tears running down our cheeks, dripping onto the floor.

I asked Simon Zhao, the man of God, "Uncle, will you please tell us more?" He continued:

> When the Lord called us to this vision, I had been married just four months. My beautiful bride had just found out she was pregnant! We were both arrested and imprisoned. Life in the prison was difficult and my wife suffered a miscarriage. In the early months of my imprisonment in 1950 I saw my beloved wife twice from afar, through the iron bars on my window. Then I never saw her again. By the time I was released many years later my precious bride was already long dead.

We all wept loudly. We felt as if we were standing on holy ground in the presence of the Lord. I asked Uncle Simon, "When you were released from prison, did you still have this Back to Jerusalem vision in your heart?"

He responded to my question by singing for us,

> How many years have bitter winds blown?
> How many times have the storm clouds gathered?
> Through the icy rain we couldn't see God's altar
> The altar of God where he accepts our sacrifices.
>
> God's leaders are crying with broken hearts
> Jehovah's sheep are scattered far and wide
> Tears of sadness well up in the chilly wind
> Where have you gone, Good Shepherd?
> Where have you gone, soldiers of God?
> Where have you gone?
> Oh, where have you gone?

After Uncle Simon had rested for a while, I asked him again, "Uncle, do you still have this vision in your heart?"

He continued to sing,

> Jerusalem is in my dreams
> Jerusalem is in my tears
> I looked for you and found you in the fire of the altar
> I looked for you and found you in Jesus' nail-scarred hands.
>
> We wandered through the valley of tears
> We wandered towards our heavenly home
> After walking through the valley of death for forty years
> My tears dried up.
>
> Jesus came to destroy the chains of death
> He came to open the path to glory!
> The early missionaries shed their blood and tears for us
> Let's hurry to fulfil the promise of God!

I held his hand and assured him, "The vision God gave you has not died! We will carry on the vision!" After we had brought comfort to the heart of Uncle Simon he stood up, blessed us with his holy hands, and encouraged us from Luke 24:46–48, *"This is what is written: The Christ will suffer and rise from the dead on the third day, and repentance and forgiveness of sins will be preached in his name to all nations, beginning at Jerusalem. You are witnesses of these things."*

He exhorted us, "You must recognize the way of the cross is the call to shed blood. You must take the gospel of Jesus Christ to the

Muslim countries, then all the way back to Jerusalem. Turn your eyes to the west!"

That meeting was a pivotal point in my life. I felt as if God passed a flaming torch from this revered old man to the house churches, giving us the responsibility to complete the vision.

The Lord had already placed the Back to Jerusalem vision in my heart, but after meeting Simon Zhao it became the primary focus of my life. I came to understand clearly that the destiny of the house churches of China is to pull down the world's last remaining spiritual strongholds—the house of Buddha, the house of Mohammed, and the house of Hinduism—and to proclaim the glorious gospel to all nations before the Second Coming of our Lord Jesus Christ!

You need to remember that when we speak about 'Back to Jerusalem' we are speaking about evangelizing the thousands of unreached people groups, towns, and villages located between China and Jerusalem. We are not ignorant of the fact that these nations don't welcome the gospel. We are well aware that countries like Afghanistan, Iran, and Saudi Arabia will not take kindly to preachers in their land!

We also understand that the missionaries we send will need to be equipped, trained with language and cultural skills, and supported so they can fight for the Lord with maximum effectiveness. Today there are hundreds of Christians inside China learning foreign languages such as Arabic and English in preparation for missionary service outside China.

But that is not the only training they have received. The past fifty years of suffering, persecution, and torture of the house churches in China were all part of God's training for us. He has used the government for his own purposes, molding and shaping his children as he sees fit. That is why I correct Western Christians who tell me: "I've been praying for years that the Communist government in China will collapse, so Christians can live in freedom." This is not what we pray! We never pray against our government or call down curses on it. Instead, we have learned that God is in control of both our own lives and the government we live under. Isaiah prophesied about Jesus, *"the government will be on his shoulders"* (Isa. 9:6). Instead of focusing our prayers against any political system, we pray that regardless of what happens to us, we will be pleasing to God.

Don't pray for the persecution to stop! We shouldn't pray for a lighter load to carry, but a stronger back to endure! Then the world will see that God is with us, empowering us to live in a way that reflects his love and power.

This is true freedom!

There is little that any of the Muslim, Buddhist, or Hindu countries can do to us that we haven't already experienced in China. The worst they can do is kill us, but all that means is we will be promoted into the glorious presence of our Lord for all eternity!

The Back to Jerusalem missionary movement is not an army with guns or human weapons. It is not a group of well-dressed, slick professionals. It is an army of broken-hearted Chinese men and women whom God has cleansed with a mighty fire, and who have already been through years of hardship and deprivation for the sake of the gospel. In worldly terms they have nothing and appear unimpressive, but in the spiritual realm they are mighty warriors for Jesus Christ!

God is calling thousands of house church warriors to write their testimonies with their own blood. We will walk across the borders of China, carrying the word of God into the Islamic, Buddhist, and Hindu worlds. Thousands will be willing to die for the Lord. They will see multitudes of souls saved, as well as awaken many sleeping churches in the West.

Hundreds of Western missionaries spilled their blood on Chinese soil in the past. Their example has inspired us to be willing to die for the Lord wherever he leads us with his message. Many of our missionaries will be captured, tortured, and martyred for the sake of the gospel, but that will not stop us. The Chinese church is willing to pay the price.

God has not only refined *us* in the fire of affliction for the past fifty years, he has also refined our methods. For example, we're totally committed to planting groups of local believers who meet in homes. We have no desire to build a single church building anywhere! This allows the gospel to spread rapidly, is harder for the authorities to detect, and enables us to channel all our resources directly into gospel ministry.

In 1997 God miraculously allowed me to escape from prison and also took me out of China for the first time in my life, so that

I might bring glory to the King of Kings before many peoples and nations. During the long flight to Germany, I thought back over my life and thanked God for his boundless grace. I know that I am the least part of the body of Christ in China. I am nothing. It's certainly not because of any special skills or abilities that God chose me to be his ambassador to the nations. It was only by his mysterious, undeserved grace.

That grace to me continued when my plane landed in Frankfurt, Germany, and I was permitted to pass through immigration and customs despite not having a passport! As I sat in a vehicle taking me to a pastor's house, the Holy Spirit powerfully spoke to my heart, "In the same way that I brought you out of prison and out of China, I will bring one hundred thousand of my children out of China to be my witnesses throughout Asia."

\* \* \*

In 2001 I journeyed to the Buddhist country of Myanmar (formerly called Burma) to fetch my family, who had managed to make their way there from China. But I was arrested as a suspected spy and was sentenced to seven years in prison. At the start of my incarceration I was almost beaten to death. I had previously tasted life inside Chinese prisons many times for the sake of the gospel, but the conditions in Myanmar were much worse than any I had experienced in China. It was literally a death factory.

While I was in prison the Lord clearly showed me that much of the ministry of Chinese missionaries in the Back to Jerusalem movement will take place in prison. Hundreds, if not thousands, will be arrested. Others will be beaten to death or executed because of the vision. The satanic hosts will do everything they can to stop our workers from going forward with the light of the gospel. But imprisonment and even death will not mean failure; they will be part of God's plan. In China we have seen on numerous occasions how revival has broken out among prisoners and guards when believers have been locked away. The revival has then spread from those dingy prison cells and has gone forth to bless many. In prison the gospel has a captive audience and men and women are usually much more receptive to the word of the Lord than they are normally.

We should not look at the Back to Jerusalem vision through human eyes. If we do, like most of the men sent to spy out the

Promised Land, all we will see are the obstacles and troubles confronting us. Chinese Christians will see that the Western church with all its wealth and strength has not been able to make much of an impact in these nations, and then we will look at ourselves and immediately give up!

Instead, we must be like Joshua and Caleb, and see Back to Jerusalem through the eyes of faith. Not man-made faith, but faith given by God. We are not going into battle because someone thinks it is a good idea. We are going into battle because we know that for more than seventy years God has been speaking to the Chinese church, telling us to take the gospel back to Jerusalem for his glory. That is why we can march forward, confident that the Commander-in-Chief will be at the head of his army.

As Back to Jerusalem gains momentum please don't judge it by a worldly standard. If you hear that hundreds of us have been killed or imprisoned, don't assume that is bad news and that the vision has failed! In China we have learned to trust the sovereignty of God. If we are in prison it is because he wants us there. The very thing some people may think a failure may turn out to be the point of breakthrough and victory.

One small example of this principle is the fact that in Myanmar I was able to lead more than a dozen prisoners to Jesus. He touched them powerfully and their lives changed forever. Some people go through their whole life free on the outside but prisoners in their hearts, enslaved to sin and bondage. These men face the most miserable existence possible inside prison, but on the inside they are as free as birds gliding over the mountaintops! They love Jesus with all their hearts. *"Therefore, I tell you, her many sins have been forgiven—for she loved much. But he who had been forgiven little loves little"* (Luke 7:47). My days in prison were filled with God's presence. To be honest, it didn't even feel as if I was in prison! I hardly even thought about the seven-year sentence I had received, for each day was so full of joy and life. Then, after seven months and seven days in prison, I was released and expelled from the country because the Lord wanted me to continue implementing the Back to Jerusalem vision.

But a far greater illustration of the principle that what looks like defeat may actually be a victory is Jesus' death on the cross. Satan and his demonic hosts thought they had won when they put to death the holy Son of God, but they could not discern the will of God. They thought they had thwarted God's plan, when in fact they had helped fulfil it! *"None of the rulers of this age understood it, for if they had, they would not have crucified the Lord of glory"* (1 Cor. 2:8).

My family and I have committed ourselves unreservedly to serve the Lord and the Back to Jerusalem movement. One day I may be killed for the sake of the gospel in a Muslim or Buddhist nation. If you hear this news, please don't grieve for me, but grieve for the millions of precious souls who are enslaved by Satan without any gospel witness. Death is not the end for a servant of God; it is just the start of indescribable everlasting life in the presence of Jesus. Please go on in my place with the gospel, preaching and discipling the people groups of the world until Jesus comes again.

- Pray that God will provide everything his children need to fulfil the Back to Jerusalem vision, *"To them God has chosen to make known among the Gentiles the glorious riches of this mystery, which is Christ in you, the hope of glory"* (Col. 1:27).

- Pray that God will give us all the spiritual and material resources we need to do his will. Ask the Lord to keep our eyes focused on Jesus at all times.

- Ask God to glorify his name through the Back to Jerusalem movement. When all is said and done, may no individual take credit for it, but may people exclaim, *"The Lord has done this, and it is marvellous in our eyes"* (Ps. 118:23).

# 6

# The Testimony of Peter Xu Yongze

*Peter Xu Yongze founded the Full Scope Church (also known as the Born Again house church movement), which has grown to approximately 20 million members in China today. Xu has long been considered the number one Christian enemy by the Chinese government, who labeled his church an "evil cult" because of his refusal to compromise and register with the authorities. He has been imprisoned for years at a time on several occasions, tortured and slandered more than any other Christian leader in China, yet he remains a faithful and humble man of God.*

Two thousand years ago, by the power of the Holy Spirit and through suffering and the shedding of blood, the gospel spread from Jerusalem to Judea, Samaria, and into the Roman Empire. It continued to spread westwards until it reached China. There, some 150 years ago, God gave Hudson Taylor a vision to preach the gospel to the inland provinces. In a way, Taylor was the one used by God to take the gospel away from the coastal areas (China's "Jerusalem") and into the interior ("Judea and Samaria"). Like a mighty soldier he marched into pioneer areas where the name of Jesus Christ had never been uttered before.

Today the house churches of China have enlarged Taylor's vision. Our aim is not only to saturate our own country with the life and presence of the Lord Jesus Christ, but also to impact all the remaining Muslim, Buddhist, and Hindu nations with the gospel. Because of God's abundant blessing, thousands of men and women have a vision from the Holy Spirit to take the gospel to the nations (the "ends of the earth") that lie between China and Jerusalem, the place where the fire of the gospel first started to spread. It is as though Hudson Taylor handed a flaming torch to the Chinese church and asked us to continue the race towards the finish line.

Another legacy from Taylor to today's Chinese church and to the Back to Jerusalem movement was his refusal to construct organizational walls that slow down the advance of the gospel and cause division among believers. He was able to cross denominational barriers and lead the body of Christ to work together under the banner of Christ, so that the church could fulfil God's vision.

Taylor was also willing to sacrifice his own comfort to spread the gospel. He cut his hair and wore a traditional Chinese cue—long braided hair, as was the custom of the day. Other missionaries considered his adherence to this custom shameful, but Taylor stubbornly refused to compromise his convictions. He also wore Chinese clothing and studied the Chinese language until he was fluent. He humbled himself to become like the people he served.

In China today, Christians still repeat Hudson Taylor's words: "If I had a thousand lives to live, I would give them all for China." Because people saw the attitude of his heart, they were attracted to his message.

After the Communists came to power in China in 1949 most church buildings were demolished. The communists thought that if they took away the places where Christians met, there would be no more Christianity. Believers were forced to meet secretly, sometimes in groups of just two or three people, and often at times like 3 o'clock in the morning, when everyone else was asleep. For years there were no pastors to shepherd the flock, no Bibles to learn from, and no hymn books to use in worship. Sometimes these tiny illegal meetings would just consist of prayer, mutual encouragement, and the taking of the Lord's Supper. Every external symbol of our faith was completely stripped away by the government, but they didn't realize that our strength didn't lie in those things anyway. Our strength lay in the one thing they could never remove—the resurrected Jesus Christ who lives in our hearts!

We soon found that rather than being weakened by the removal of all external props, we were actually much stronger because our faith in God was purer. We didn't have any opportunity to love the "things" of God, so we just learned to love God! We had no plans or programs to keep running, so we just sought the face of Jesus! We had no opportunity to make money, so we spent all our time making disciples!

In the 1970s and early 1980s, we were all one church. There were no significant theological differences between us and no blockages to our fellowship. We had all been deeply touched by God's Spirit. We went to prison together, were beaten together, and bled together. We also preached the gospel together.

But by the early 1990s many leaders who were once close brothers in the work of the gospel had become critical of each other. We had always stated that we in China would never form denominations like those in the Western church, yet we had all gone different ways and built walls between us. The Back to Jerusalem vision had been present for many years, but the house churches were not yet ready to fulfil this call. The Lord knew we could never be effective in our witness to Muslims, Buddhists, and Hindus while we remained weak and divided.

God used Brother Yun to bring unity among the leaders of various house church networks. This was no easy task for years of silence between us had created unseen walls of bitterness and hostility. Many house church leaders believed their group possessed the truth and that other groups had gone astray and drifted into error. When Brother Yun first spoke to us about unity, he got a cold reception.

But God performed a series of miracles that led to a meeting of the leaders of several house church networks in 1996. It was the first time many of us had seen each other for years. At that first meeting the Lord broke through our stubbornness and pride and there were many tears of repentance. We all confessed our bitterness to each other and asked for forgiveness.

I stood up in the first unity meeting and said, "We don't want to follow our own pet doctrines any more. We want to learn from one another's strengths and change in whatever way the Lord wants us to change in order to make us stronger and closer to Jesus."[39]

Although not all differences were ironed out, the leaders came to appreciate their fellow leaders and saw they had far more in common than they had reasons to remain separate. They also found that their theological differences centerd on things that weren't essential to the faith.

Each group clearly heard how God was moving in wonderful ways among the other groups represented in the meeting and gave glory to God. We decided to speak in each other's churches and to share Bibles and resources between us so that one or two groups would not end up receiving the majority of the help from overseas Christians, while other groups got nothing.

On the second day, all the leaders took communion together. It was the first time in more than fifty years that the leaders of China's church had taken the Lord's Supper in unity.

I believe that meeting in 1996, and the ones that followed, were some of the most important events in the history of Christianity in China, because the Back to Jerusalem movement would never have gotten off the ground while the house churches remained divided. It was no coincidence that it was after 1996 that the details of the Back to Jerusalem vision began to fall into place.

> *How good and pleasant it is when brothers live together in unity! It is like precious oil poured on the head, running down on the beard, running down upon Aaron's beard, down upon the collar of his robes. It is as if the dew of Hermon were falling on Mount Zion. For there the Lord bestows his blessing, even life forevermore.* (Ps. 133:1–3)

When we talk of this unity, it needs to be understood that the reason we came together was not for the sake of unity in itself. It was unity for the sake of fulfilling the common vision God had given us—the vision of taking the gospel back to Jerusalem, thus completing the Great Commission and hastening the return of our Lord! That is why we started our unified gatherings. Although various house churches still have different interpretations of some Scriptures and different practices, we recognize that we all share the common goal of sharing the good news with every person inside China and beyond.

When believers are united around a common goal, we can head there together, putting aside our petty differences. When we lose sight of our common vision, we stop looking forward and begin to look at each other. Soon we see each other's weaknesses and faults, and instead of fighting for the kingdom of God we start fighting each other.

It's quite simple to tell a strong church from a weak one. A strong church is one that is a spiritual baby-making center. Souls are being saved and discipled around the clock and the church is a hive of activity. There is no time for believers to sit around and argue with each other. They are too busy just trying to clean up all the mess these newborn babies make while simultaneously trying to prepare more bottles of milk to keep them fed! As the father of two small children, I well know what a struggle this can be!

Some churches are full of people who think it is their calling to keep other people in line so that they don't get polluted by the world. This may sound like spiritual activity, and the people who make the most noise about it may look pious, but if their words produce no spiritual life, it is all a waste of time. It is far better for us to concentrate on preaching the gospel and let God police his church.

Sometimes foreign Christians visit the house churches in China and make comments like, "The church in China is extraordinary."

This is not true.

"Normal" Christianity for a believer is surely when we live according to the pattern of the church laid out in the word of God. The church in the Book of Acts did not have remarkable experiences and success, they had what should be normal lives and experiences for any church that claims to have been redeemed by the precious blood of Jesus! They were the standard for us to follow. Much of the church in the world today, including in China, is abnormal and unbiblical. May we all fall to our knees and seek the Lord's help to live out what he accepts as normal Christianity!

While he was dealing with the Chinese church and purifying us, God put the vision for Back to Jerusalem deep into the hearts of the house church leadership. He showed us that spiritual life should be the foundation of our Christianity, building up the church is the center, and the training of workers is the point of breakthrough—the strategic place from where expansion can be carried out in all directions, radiating to every nation and people in the world, so that the ground that the soles of our feet walk on will become our inheritance! As we implement this strategy through all the nations that have until now resisted the claims of our lovely Lord Jesus, we will see individuals and families having their eyes opened to the gospel by the power of the Holy Spirit *"that you may declare the praises of him who called you out of darkness and into his wonderful light"* (1 Pet. 2:9).

The power for Back to Jerusalem will have to come from the Holy Spirit. I have spent much time meditating on the following verse:

> *Can plunder be taken from warriors, or captives rescued from the fierce? But this is what the Lord says: "Yes, captives will be taken from warriors,*

*and plunder retrieved from the fierce; I will contend with those who contend with you, and your children I will save. I will make your oppressors eat their own flesh; they will be drunk on their own blood, as with wine. Then all mankind will know that I, the Lord, am your Savior, your Redeemer, the Mighty One of Jacob."* (Isa. 49:24–25)

I have come to understand that it is completely impossible for even a single lost person in the world to become a Christian unless a great miracle takes place. Lost human souls are firmly chained prisoners of Satan and his demonic forces. They cannot be argued into the kingdom of God because their problem is not an intellectual one. Nor is there any point in trying to change their outward behavior if they do not have the inward spiritual life that only Jesus can give. The Bible clearly says that every person outside of Christ is spiritually dead, and a battle needs to be waged for his or her soul. People living outside the grace of Jesus Christ are trapped by the devil, *"who has taken them captive to do his will"* (2 Tim. 2:26).

The demonic forces that hold souls captive are far more powerful than we are, in our own strength. There is not the slightest possibility that we can lead anyone to the foot of the cross unless Jesus himself becomes involved. Only his power can save a sinner. The good news is that we can be completely sure that Jesus will help us to reach the lost for him, for the word of God says, *"He is patient with you, not wanting anyone to perish, but everyone to come to repentance"* (2 Pet. 3:9).

God will move in great power to *"retrieve plunder from the fierce"* (Isa. 49:24) because each person who puts their faith and trust in Jesus brings glory and honor to God's holy name and magnifies the wonderful victory Jesus purchased for mankind by his death on the cross. It is only when Jesus gets involved with our lives and ministry that we will start to see others come to know him. Jesus asked, *"How can anyone enter a strong man's house and carry off his possessions unless he first ties up the strong man? Then he can rob his house"* (Matt. 12:29). It is only when we learn to walk hand in hand with our Heavenly Father that the strongman who dominates the lives of people and whole nations will be bound.

I have complete confidence that the Lord will help us as we take the gospel back to Jerusalem. His bride will be prepared for the wedding feast in heaven that Jesus mentioned when he said, *"I say to you that many will come from the east and the west, and will take their places at the feast with Abraham, Isaac, and Jacob in the kingdom of heaven"* (Matt. 8:11).

This is surely the time to complete the Great Commission that God gave his followers two thousand years ago. If God had only wanted to save us, he would take us to heaven the moment we believed in him. Instead, he leaves his unworthy children on this earth for a reason, to proclaim the good news to all the nations of the world that Jesus is alive and has come to set the captives free! Let's devote all our heart, time, and energy to his purpose. Let Back to Jerusalem become the reason we live.

The Lord has led my wife and I to dedicate the rest of our lives to seeing the Back to Jerusalem vision become a reality. We have much to learn. Recently God led us to leave China so that we could be more closely involved with the Back to Jerusalem mission. Outside China we can be involved with training, strategizing, and planning much more freely than we could be when we were inside China. But we have to avoid distractions! Since we left China many well-meaning Christians have invited us to come and speak at this meeting and that meeting, but we have learned to say "no" unless the meeting is directly related to the vision to which God has called us.

We greatly miss our co-workers and the close fellowship of our brothers and sisters, but at the same time we are excited as we believe Back to Jerusalem is the destiny of the church in China. Perhaps we will see you along the Silk Road as you join with us in evangelizing all the nations of the world for Jesus!

Oh, how these unreached nations—who do not know God but worship idols—need the gospel of Jesus Christ! Now is God's time for us to wake up. We must humbly repent and be alert, watch and pray! By the power of the Holy Spirit we will be able to defeat the strongholds of evil and pierce stubborn hearts, so that people will come to the Lord.

I would like to ask you to please pray for the Back to Jerusalem movement in the following ways:

- Pray that the Lord will give many more Christians the vision to take the gospel Back to Jerusalem.

- Pray that we will be fully prepared for a battle to the death. I believe that we are facing the greatest spiritual war the church has seen. The stakes are high! Success means nothing less than the fulfilment of the Great Commission and the return of our Lord Jesus Christ! The devil, who has kept Muslim, Buddhist and Hindu nations captive for thousands of years, will not surrender without a strong and bloody fight. *"A curse on him who is lax in doing the Lord's work! A curse on him who keeps his sword from bloodshed!"* (Jer. 48:10)

- Pray that God will find his church faithful to obey the calling he has given us to take the gospel to all the unreached nations of the world.

# 7

# The Testimony of Enoch Wang

*Enoch Wang is one of the leaders of a Christian movement that sprang from Watchman Nee's teaching. Today it numbers millions of believers throughout China. Brother Enoch has spent 16 of the last 20 years in prison for the sake of the gospel. Just a few months after giving this interview, he was arrested again. This key leader of the Chinese church talks about what the Back to Jerusalem movement means to him and shares a remarkable personal testimony that is well known and verified by many church leaders in China.*

I first became a Christian in 1969—during the Cultural Revolution—when I was a leader of the Communist Red Guards. My faith in God was shallow for the first year. In 1970 I actually became a member of the Communist Party, even though I was also a believer in Christ! Soon I was promoted to the leadership of the Communist Youth League, and in 1972 I was assigned to work in a People's Liberation Army weapons factory. It wasn't until 1973 that I really got serious about serving the Lord Jesus.

I was first sent to prison from 1982 to 1994 because of my faith in God. They hated the fact that an atheist Red Guard and a leader of the Communist Youth League was now a Christian pastor! In all those years they tried to break me and make me turn away from the Lord, but by God's grace they could not remove the deposit of God in my heart.

When I was arrested our little daughter was just three years old. It was painful to be separated from my wife and child, but I hoped our local Christians would take care of them in my absence. The authorities knew this, so they decided to watch my family to see if they received any outside assistance. I had been sentenced as a counter-revolutionary and a traitor—the very worst crimes in China. Anyone found trying to help the family of a counter-revolutionary is accused of the same crime, and so fear of punishment resulted in my Christian brothers and sisters being unable to help my family.

We lived on a farm but my wife didn't know how to plant and

harvest the crops, so my family soon began to starve and went through a time of incredible hardship. During the first summer, my wife tried to harvest the corn in our fields while my daughter stayed at home. When she was just four years old she learned how to cook so she could help her mother! She even learned how to start a fire and boil water for noodles, as well as how to cook simple meals.

The pressure on our little girl was intense. No child should ever have to face the type of life she did, but the Lord helped them and today my daughter is a beautiful young woman who serves the Lord with all her heart.

After I was transferred to a prison labor camp in a different part of our province, my wife and daughter also moved to that town so they could continue to visit me. For years my dear wife raised our daughter all alone, with no Christian fellowship, no husband and no money. Sometimes they scavenged through garbage cans looking for scraps of food to eat or some item they could sell at the market for a few cents. At other times they were forced to beg. On one occasion, when she was at her lowest point, God gave her a vision of paradise that encouraged her faith and helped her to carry on.

Many Christians around the world pray for pastors in China when they are sent to prison, and for this we are deeply grateful. However, please remember to pray also for the families of those pastors, as often their ordeal is even worse than that of those in prison. After all, I at least got a couple of coarse meals each day.

Visits from my family were bitter-sweet experiences. They never complained about their lives, but their skinny, malnourished bodies revealed their desperate struggle. I longed to see them and was encouraged when they came. But the pain of knowing what they were experiencing was the worst form of persecution the authorities could give me.

My daughter could not attend school because we had no money for books or a school uniform. Also, children of "counter-revolutionaries" were ridiculed and harassed by teachers and other students. Since my release from prison the believers in our church got together and decided to send her to university to make up for the years in which she missed out on education. The Lord has helped her and this year she graduated.

When I was finally released in 1994, I thought we would have a joyous reunion but I didn't fully understand what my wife and daughter had been through all those years. A lot of the emotions and pain that had built up over 13 years came flooding out. My wife and I had to start our relationship all over again. Only by the gracious help of our Lord Jesus did we progress. Now everything is fine and I am deeply grateful to the Lord for having given me such a wonderful helpmate. Without her I couldn't do anything! God has always been good to us.

When I went to prison I thought that my own church was correct in doctrine and practice and that the other house church groups in China had serious errors. Accordingly in the early years I had little or no contact with other parts of Christ's body in China, believing I was serving God by avoiding all contact with them. It was only after being released that I learned to have God's heart for all his children.

In 1997, just when our family life was becoming more settled, I was arrested again and spent three more years in prison. That was the same occasion when Brother Yun and Brother Xu were arrested, as well as many other house church leaders. I was in prison when God miraculously allowed Yun to escape, even though his legs had been beaten so badly that he was known as "the cripple." God supernaturally opened the doors for Yun to escape. I am a witness to the fact that *"what he opens no one can shut, and what he shuts no one can open"* (Rev. 3:7).

I would like to share one part of my testimony that directly relates to the Back to Jerusalem vision.

In 1995 my wife and I had another little girl. I was 45 years old and not expecting to be a father again. The Bible says, *"Sons are a heritage from the Lord, children a reward from him"* (Ps. 127:3). We were so happy.

On New Year's Day 1997 a unity meeting was organized by Brother Yun near my home town. Leaders of various house church networks were invited to attend so that we could all have fellowship with one another, pray together, and break down the barriers that existed between different groups. I was eager to attend because the Lord had been showing me that unity within the house church movement was essential if we were to advance with the gospel as God intended.

Until we truly forgave each other and were reconciled, I knew that God would never fully bless our work.

At that time my family was being hunted by the police. We were living in a fourth-floor apartment in a building that was still under construction. We couldn't get a normal place because doing so would have required us to register with the local authorities, which would have led to our immediate arrest.

On the very morning that I was to travel to the unity meeting, I was talking on the telephone when I heard screaming. My wife burst into the bedroom shouting hysterically. My eldest daughter, who was 18 years old, had been holding her baby sister, 15 months old at the time, on the balcony overlooking the street. Somehow our baby girl managed to slip out of her sister's grasp. She fell four stories and landed, head first, on a pile of bricks on the street below.

My wife was holding our baby daughter in her arms and crying. She said, "Hurry, we must take her to the hospital at once!" I immediately saw that the baby was dead. Her head was smashed and a small piece of white brain tissue was protruding through the front of her skull.

I said, "There's no point going to the hospital. She is already dead. There is nothing the hospital can do to make her any better." An array of emotions went through me. On one hand I knew she was dead, so there was no need to go to the hospital. I also knew that if we went to the hospital the authorities would soon find out we were not registered, and I would be arrested and sent back to prison, quite probably on charges of murdering my own baby. We would be in trouble for living illegally in an unfinished building, and the family who gave us permission to live there would also be in trouble.

I also felt that this incident was a direct demonic attack, intended to distract my attention and prevent my co-workers and me from attending the vital unity meeting. Satan is not happy when God's people come together to break down barriers between them. He had spent years slyly building walls of unforgiveness, misunderstanding, and prejudice. It was not surprising that he would throw all his efforts into preventing the meeting from taking place.

I knelt down and prayed. I was angry, shocked, and in grief, all at the same time. I said, "Lord, if it is your will for the church in China to be unified, then I pray you will bring my daughter back to life.

I pray that today you will put the breath of life back in her body, tomorrow you will allow her to speak, and the day after tomorrow she will be able to walk. But if it is not your will for the church in China to be unified, then I will hide myself and will never preach your gospel again." Of course I would always continue to believe in the Lord, but I would remove myself from the front lines and would just lead a quiet, peaceful life.

Some people might say I had no right to speak to God like that, but you need to understand I was in deep shock and I knew this accident had been a deliberate demonic action designed to stop me attending the unity meeting.

My wife continued to hold our baby in her arms and rock the lifeless body back and forth. Our beautiful daughter had completely stopped breathing, her heart was not beating and she was pale.

The meeting was due to begin that evening in a location about 20 miles away from my home. I decided to put my grief aside and attend the meeting as a sign of defiance of Satan and an act of faith in God. I also decided not to cry, even though I was deeply grieved in my heart. I wanted to show the devil that he could never intimidate or stop me.

In the late afternoon I left my home and made my way to the meeting, well wrapped up against the cool winter air. When I left home my wife was still holding the baby in her arms and weeping. The piece of brain was still exposed, sticking out of a crack in her skull. My eldest daughter was devastated, blaming herself for having dropped her sister from the balcony.

When I got to the meeting, Brother Yun was already speaking. My co-workers and I took our seats and didn't tell any of the other believers what had happened. During the evening meal we chose not to eat. Instead we fasted and prayed together in the meeting room, but I still didn't tell anyone else what had happened. I reminded the Lord what a blessing our little girl was, and how much delight her birth had brought to me at the age of 45. I examined my heart to see if this had happened because of any sin in me. I told the Lord if it had happened because I had offended him, then I would have nothing to complain about. *"Shall we accept good from God, and not trouble? . . . . The Lord gave and the Lord has taken away; may the name of the Lord be praised"* (Job 2:10, 1:21).

After the first day's meetings concluded, I knew my family needed me so I returned home where I found my wife and elder daughter still weeping. Their eyes were red and swollen. My wife was still holding the dead baby in her arms. I leaned forward and prayed over my baby in the name of Jesus Christ. Suddenly I heard a small kind of gasping noise come from her mouth, like a small burp. I realized that she must be breathing and I cried out, "Praise be to God!"

All four of us slept in the same bedroom, but that night none of us got any sleep. Emotionally drained, we just sat there praying quietly. At five o'clock I got up and went back to the unity meeting and spent the whole day in prayer and discussion with the other house church leaders, who were still ignorant of what had happened. At ten o'clock in the evening the meeting ended for the day and I again returned home.

When I entered the door of our home I found a different atmosphere. Despair had turned into joy. My wife was breast-feeding my little daughter. She was breathing fine, the color had returned to her cheeks, and she was hungry! God had miraculously healed her skull, and skin had covered the part of her brain that had been exposed. No medical help had been given her, except that of the great physician, Jesus. All that remained of her fall was a small scar in the middle of her forehead.

Despite these obvious improvements, she was still far from normal. She could not walk or move, her eyes were closed, and she just lay there almost motionless except for breathing and sucking.

I called out her name, "Sheng Ling", which means "spiritual blessing." When she heard my voice she stopped drinking her milk and a small sound came from her mouth, as if she were greeting me. That night I was able to sleep soundly, knowing the Lord was doing a great miracle.

The next morning I again awoke early and made my way to the third day of the meetings. There was much repentance and confession by the leaders of various groups. We heard many hours of testimonies about how God was working in each house church network, and we all realized that the Lord was with those other groups just as much as he was with us. Many years of bitterness and division came tumbling down at the foot of the cross. Tears flowed as we embraced one another and accepted each other as true brothers and sisters in Christ. Satan was furious that we were sitting together as God's people. He wanted us to continue to work separately, weakened by dividing walls. Jesus' desire is that his children will walk together. He prayed in John 17:22–23,

> I have given them the glory that you gave me, that they may be one as we are one: I in them and you in me. May they be brought to complete unity to let the world know that you sent me and have loved them even as you have loved me.

I believe that without this meeting, and others like it, there would be no unity among the different branches of China's house church today. In our previous splintered state there would have been no way we could ever have hoped to obey God's call to take the gospel through the Muslim, Buddhist, and Hindu nations back to Jerusalem. This is why I want to share this personal testimony, as for me it was a pivotal moment in my own understanding and involvement with the Back to Jerusalem movement.

When I returned home on the third night, my wife was again breast-feeding my daughter. I held out my arms and said, "Sheng Ling, come and let your daddy hold you." She took one step towards me and then toppled over, but we all rejoiced that she had taken that one step. Just two days before she had been dead with her brain sticking out of her smashed skull. I started to cry with joy.

It was on this third night that I told my family what I had prayed when Sheng Ling first fell out of the window. I told them, "When you first brought her body up from the street, I knelt down and said to God, 'I pray you will bring my daughter back to life. I pray that today you will put the breath of life back in her body, tomorrow you will allow her to speak, and the day after tomorrow she will be able to walk.'"

When they heard this they rejoiced greatly, knowing God had done a great miracle.

On the fourth morning I went to the meeting with overwhelming joy in my heart. My enthusiasm was soon dampened when a number of house church leaders pointed at me and said, "Those attending this important meeting are expected to stay here. What kind of commitment do you have to unity if you can't even stay with us, but have to go hurrying home as soon as the meeting ends every night?"

I still hadn't shared any information with the other leaders at the meeting, so they had no idea what had been going on in my life.

In the final session of the meeting Brother Yun was scheduled to speak, then the leaders intended to pray together one last time before everyone dispersed back to their homes. While he was speaking, my eldest daughter came into the room and started to whisper excitedly into my ear. She had hurried to the meeting place to tell me that her little sister was now walking and talking normally! It was at that stage that I felt compelled to stand up. I declared to everyone, "Now I know that it is God's will for the church in China to be unified!" Before more than one hundred leaders, I testified about what had happened to my baby daughter. Everyone praised God. Those who had criticized me for going home every night came up and apologized.

Not only did the Lord heal Sheng Ling from the fall, but he has blessed her in a very special way. She is now eight years old and is so smart that her school made her skip a year ahead of her classmates! She has suffered no long-term damage as a result of her fall. The only thing that remains is the small scar on her forehead. It is as though the Lord left the scar to remind us of his great grace and power.

You are welcome to come and visit us any time! You will see that Sheng Ling is a bright and energetic little girl who loves the Lord with all her heart. Her name "Spiritual Blessing" suits her.

The Lord first started speaking to me about taking the gospel back to Jerusalem in 1979. Since then, it has gradually become the main purpose for my serving the Lord. It is the commission I have from the Lord, his calling to me.

- Please pray that the church in China will know God's will so that we will offer ourselves to God without reservation or hesitation. Pray for more and more believers in China to have this burden to take the gospel back to Jerusalem.

- Pray that we will be able to work together with believers from all around the world so that we can complete the Great Commission together. When all nations have received a gospel witness, the end shall come.

# 8

# Strategies

*Trust in the Lord with all your heart and lean not on your
own understanding; in all your ways acknowledge him, and
he will make your paths straight.*

*— Proverbs 3:5–6*

When we talk about strategies for implementing the Back to
Jerusalem vision, let us clarify from the beginning that we have no
desire to sit down and make our own plans. We only want to hear the
voice of God and not human opinions, for we know that when the
Lord reveals his will to us and we obey, our mission will be a success
regardless of the results. Success is obeying God. Failure is when we
don't obey God.

The Lord has revealed several fundamental strategies relating to
the Back to Jerusalem vision that we would like to share here. Please
pray that God will give us his wisdom in all things, so that the whole
movement will be rooted in his will and operated in his strength. We
desire to be like the *"men of Issachar, who understood the times and knew
what Israel should do"* (1 Chron. 12:32).

## The Route

Although China is a long, long way from Jerusalem, one of the
remarkable facts of history is that Jerusalem has been connected
to China by road for more than two millennia. The long-reigning
Emperor Wudi (138–87 B.C.) is credited with opening up the Silk
Road.

Some accounts suggest the gospel may first have entered China
down this road just a few decades after Jesus' death and resurrection.
Seven centuries ago the famous explorer Marco Polo came to China
along the same highway. This key trading route allowed herbs and
spices, treasure, new religions, and invading armies to flow in and

out of China. At the other end, Jerusalem acted as a hub from where products dispersed into Europe, North Africa, and the Middle East.

The route takes its name from a humble creature from China— the silkworm. European aristocrats were amazed when they first imported the fabric made from the fiber spun by this worm, and the subsequent trade in silk fabric gave this rugged route its name.

Today, the nations along the ancient Silk Road are the most unevangelized in the world. The three great religious strongholds that have refused to yield to the advance of the gospel—Islam, Buddhism, and Hinduism—have their heart here. More than ninety per cent of the remaining unreached people groups in the world live along the Silk Road and in the nations surrounding China. Two billion of the earth's inhabitants live and die in this area, completely oblivious to the good news that Jesus died for their sins and is the only way to heaven!

While most people have heard about "the" Silk Road, few are aware that in actual fact there were several Silk Roads in Chinese history. The main route started at China's ancient capital city of Xian and went all the way to Jerusalem and beyond. There was also a southern route that went through southwest China (where the majority of today's ethnic minority people groups are located) into Southeast Asia, entering at two main points into Vietnam and Myanmar (Burma). Goods transported along the southern route often found their way to Jerusalem and Europe by ultimately connecting to the main Silk Road through Central Asia and the Middle East.

Another trading route commenced at the city of Chengdu in Sichuan Province and passed through Lhasa and southward into the nation of Bhutan, also cutting across parts of today's northern India and Nepal—the heart of the Tibetan Buddhist and Hindu worlds. This Silk Road, too, ultimately connected with the main Silk Road linking China and Jerusalem. Other lesser-known trading routes have existed since ancient times, including sea routes. By the Tang Dynasty (A.D. 618–907), China had an advanced maritime system with ocean-going ships travelling as far away as the east coast of Africa.

When the house church leaders of China discovered that there were several different Silk Roads, we felt that this clarified our Back to Jerusalem call. Not only were we meant to go westward through the Muslim world, we were also called to take the gospel to the ethnic minorities in Southwest China and the nations of Southeast Asia. Our vision also includes the North Asian countries of Japan, North Korea, and Mongolia. In fact, many of our brothers and sisters have a deep burden from God to become missionaries to these three countries, and many are already laboring there today.

The Holy Spirit has already called certain church networks to focus on specific areas. For example, one network has many missionary families already working in Tibetan areas. It will be natural for them to lead the thrust into the Tibetan Buddhist world. Another network has for years had a burden to reach the minority groups in southwest China. Most of these tribes spill across borders into countries like Vietnam, Laos, Thailand, and Myanmar. That network has assumed responsibility for taking the gospel back to Jerusalem via the southern route.

# The Workers

We will be sending out our best workers as Back to Jerusalem missionaries. It would be foolish for an army to send its youngest, most inexperienced soldiers to the front line of a battle. In the same way, we will be sending our best equipped, most experienced workers to the front lines in the march back to Jerusalem.

When deciding who should be part of the first team to be sent out from China in 2000, we looked for those who had been in leadership positions within the house churches for at least ten years, who had suffered much hardship for the kingdom of God, and whose ministries had produced much fruit over time. The first 39 workers were tough gospel warriors. They had to be. Thirty-six of them were arrested in their first few days as missionaries!

When the house churches heard about the arrest of 36 of the 39 workers, do you think they were disillusioned? Far from it! Believers all around the nation lifted up holy hands before the Lord and with tears streaming down their cheeks they thanked the Lord for performing the great miracle of getting three Chinese missionaries out of China! We have learned to be thankful for any advance of the gospel.

All of those arrested returned home for a short time, prayed more, and then retraced the route to the countries God had called them to minister in.

Two different kinds of workers have been, and will be, part of the Back to Jerusalem movement. The first kind will leave China for relatively short periods, up to a year at a time. They will preach the gospel and serve the Lord however he directs for a time, before returning to China to await the next command from the Lord. The second kind of workers will be like Abraham. They will move from their homes and relocate to wherever God shows them and will not come back to China unless the Holy Spirit directs them to.

Jesus also sent out short-term and long-term missionaries. He gave each group very different instructions because their callings were so different. To the short-term group of twelve apostles, Jesus said, *"Take nothing for the journey—no staff, no bag, no bread, no money, no extra tunic. Whatever house you enter, stay there until you leave that town. If people do not welcome you, shake the dust off your feet as a testimony against them"* (Luke 9:3–5).

Later, however, during their Last Supper together, Jesus knew he would soon leave the disciples and wanted them to go out as his ambassadors to the nations of the world. This time Jesus was sending them out for long-term service. He asked, *"'When I sent you without purse, bag, and sandals, did you lack anything?' 'Nothing,' they answered. He said to them, 'But now if you have a purse, take it, and also a bag; and if you don't have a sword, sell your cloak and buy one'"* (Luke 22:35–36).

Just as Jesus trained his disciples, so each Back to Jerusalem missionary receives training in a number of areas. These include:

1. *How to reach across cultural and other barriers.* Our missionaries receive training in cross-cultural communication.

2. *How to reach specific groups.* Those who are going to work in Islamic areas are trained in how to effectively reach Muslims. Those targeting Buddhists are taught how Buddhist people view the world. The Lord is asked to reveal his strategy for each worker.

3. *How to suffer and die for the Lord.* We examine what the Bible says about suffering, and look at how the Lord's people have laid down their lives for the advance of the gospel throughout history.

4. *How to witness for the Lord.* We teach how to witness for the Lord under any circumstance, on trains or buses or even in the back of a police van on the way to execution.

5. *How to escape.* We know that sometimes the Lord sends us to prison to witness for him, but we also believe that the devil sometimes wants us imprisoned to stop the ministry God has called us to do. We teach the missionaries special skills such as how to free themselves from handcuffs within 30 seconds and how to jump from second-story windows without injuring themselves.

This is not a 'normal' seminary or Bible college! Should you ever visit us, you may see people with their hands tied behind their backs leaping from second-story windows. We are serious about fulfilling our destiny in God. Nothing less is required if we are to break down the walls that keep Muslims, Hindus, and Buddhists from knowing the sweet presence of Jesus.

## The Team

In the military, some soldiers undertake long-term strategic service while others are given short-term missions such as taking a piece of land or establishing a beachhead. Some are commanders, others planners and support personnel. There are many different roles, but none is more important than another. All must be diligently performed for the army to fulfil its duty. The same is true of the Back to Jerusalem movement. There will be leaders, trainers, intercessors, and facilitators. There will also be a team of pastors dedicated to taking care of the spiritual and physical needs of both long-term and short-term field workers.

Our strategy is also not to send individuals or couples somewhere to reach the lost. We will send teams of workers. This strategy is based on the pattern in the New Testament ministries of Jesus, the Apostle Paul, and others. There are many advantages to having a team, especially in spiritually dark places without any Christian presence. When part of a team, workers always have others to offer them fellowship and encouragement, and to hold them accountable. Resources, too, can be shared. We have seen over many years that sending out teams produces far greater fruitfulness than sending scattered individuals.

God wants us to work in teams, not alone. Jesus had a team, Moses had a team, David had a team, and Paul had many people work with him on teams.

The Apostle Paul's teams were a mix of people with different ethnic and occupational backgrounds. For example, his teams included

- Paul, a Jewish scholar and tentmaker by occupation (see Acts 18:3)

- Priscilla and Aquila, olive-skinned Italians (Acts 18:2)

- Luke, a doctor (Col. 4:14)

- Christians from Cyrene (in today's Libya, Africa) (Acts 11:19–21). In those days, centuries before the spread of Islam, these Christians from Cyrene were most likely dark-skinned

- Aristarchus and Gaius, from Macedonia in Asia Minor (Acts 19:29)

- Zenas, who was a lawyer (Titus 3:13), and

- Onesimus, a slave (Phil. 10)

Imagine the impact of a team like this arriving in a town to preach the gospel! Brown, white and black people who loved and served each other despite their physical, cultural, and linguistic differences. Unified teams of men and women from different occupational backgrounds ranging from doctors and lawyers to slaves. What a powerful witness to a divided and lost world!

History shows us that when people become isolated and inbred, they get genetic defects and grow weak. The same principle applies to the church. When we work with other people and churches, we allow ourselves to learn from their different ideas and our mutual strong points surface. God loves the exchange of ideas, because we glean from each other's strengths and the Body of Christ grows stronger as a result.

Even though God has given the specific Back to Jerusalem vision to the Chinese church, he has also brought along various non-Chinese believers to serve our vision, to advise us, provide research, train our workers in cross-cultural communication, encourage us, and work hand in hand with us. We have had Arab Christians come to China and teach us how to more effectively reach Muslims with the gospel. Tibetan believers have come down from the Tibetan plateau to tell the house churches what mistakes we were unknowingly making in our outreach to Tibetan Buddhists. Foreign brothers and sisters have come and shared their vision with us. Each of these contacts has opened our minds and spirits to a larger world beyond our own.

We are open and ready to receive believers whose motives are pure and whose skills and giftings are sent by the Lord to help us to more effectively

> *prepare God's people for works of service, so that the body of Christ may be built up until we all reach unity in the faith and in the knowledge of the Son of God and become mature, attaining to the whole measure of the fullness of Christ. . . . From him the whole body, joined and held together by every supporting ligament, grows and builds itself up in love, as each part does its work.* (Eph. 4:11–13, 16)

# Money

We knew from the beginning that the cost of this Back to Jerusalem mission will be high. And I'm not just talking about money! Many Christians will be martyred and suffer as this vision unfolds. Many will go on one-way tickets, realizing they will never return to China to see their loved ones again.

We also realize that it will cost a lot of money. Even though our churches are very poor, we have already collected tens of thousands of dollars to support our missionaries. Like the Macedonian church, many Chinese believers have given literally all they own, *"Out of the most severe trial, their overflowing joy and their extreme poverty welled up in rich generosity. For I testify that they gave as much as they were able, and even beyond their ability"* (2 Cor. 8:2–3).

We are often asked how we are going to finance the Back to Jerusalem movement. The answer is simple: we aren't! But we believe that God will, and that he has done so until now. We don't know where the finances to send out and sustain all of these workers will come from, but we can tell you that we look to the hand of God for his provision and not to human hands. If someone wants to give to this vision, we are far more interested in whether their hearts are connected to us than in their gift.

Map 4. This map shows the main trading routes that have linked China with the rest of the world since ancient times. The Chinese church plans to send at least 100,000 missionaries along these same routes as part of the Back to Jerusalem movement.

We are thus not concerned about where the finances will come from for Back to Jerusalem. It is the Lord's responsibility to provide and not ours. For decades we have seen him miraculously provide for the work in China. We could fill many books with accounts of what he has done.

Here is just one testimony that comes to mind. In the late 1980s two young Christian teenage girls from Henan Province were called by the Lord to travel across the country to remote Qinghai Province to share the gospel with the unreached Tu and Mongolian ethnic minorities who live there. They had no financial support, no return ticket and no contacts. The whole region was completely devoid of the gospel. After arriving among these people, their hearts were filled with compassion and they tried to share Christ's message, but the local women opposed them and drove them out of their homes. They were forced to sleep wherever they could find shelter, under bushes, in farm sheds, and the like. They were struggling, their stomachs were empty, and nobody would listen to the good news they had brought with them. They were in a position where unless the Lord did a miracle, they would die.

The Lord never abandons his children in their time of need! One day the two girls heard about an unused cave the locals avoided because they believed it to be haunted by demons. The girls saw this as the Lord's provision and prayed against any unclean spirits as they moved into their new home. But even here they were harassed. Many nights they were scared by the sounds of what they thought was a pack of wolves outside. Later they learned that the sounds came from a group of young boys who were trying to frighten them.

Winter came and temperatures plummeted to below freezing. These were particularly testing times because the people refused to open their doors to the girls. The girls prayed for many hours with tears in their eyes, asking the Lord to help them. One night they were particularly downcast and hungry. They again prayed until they fell asleep. In the morning they awoke to find that during the night mushrooms had grown right outside the entrance of their cave! They picked them and immediately boiled them, thanking God for their nutritious meal.

The next morning they woke to find the mushrooms had grown up again during the night! This continued every morning for about a year! Even in winter these miraculous mushrooms never failed to appear, poking their heads up through the snow outside the entrance to the cave. The girls learned how to enjoy mushrooms in every possible way. They boiled them, fried them and steamed them! They always tasted delicious because they knew they were gifts directly from the Lord.

Gradually these two young sisters started to be accepted by the local community and one by one they were able to lead local women to Christ, until they had a small fellowship for the first time in the history of these minority groups. After about a year, one of the young women secured a job as a dishwasher in a local restaurant. The very same day she commenced work, the mushrooms stopped appearing outside the cave!

For many years now the "haunted" cave has been used as a Bible training center for the new believers. Now hundreds of people have come to Christ in that area.

When we serve God it's important to concentrate on his character and our obedience to his leading. When we do this we won't be concerned and burdened in any way, for we know the resources are always there to do what God tells a Christian to do. As Hudson Taylor taught, "God's work, done in God's way, will never lack God's supply." He didn't only teach these words, he proved them true by his life. We saw and learned.

We also see this truth at work in the life of Elijah:

> Then the word of the Lord came to Elijah: "Leave here, turn eastward and hide in the Kerith Ravine, east of the Jordan." . . . So he [Elijah] did what the Lord had told him. He went to the Kerith Ravine, east of the Jordan, and stayed there. The ravens brought him bread and meat in the morning and bread and meat in the evening, and he drank from the brook. (1 Kgs. 17:2–6)

When the Lord tells us to do something he always provides.

Soon after this experience, however, Elijah was intimidated by the threats of Jezebel and fled into the desert. The Lord didn't tell him to go there, but the Bible records, "Elijah was afraid and ran for his life . . . a day's journey into the desert." In deep depression, Elijah complained, "I have had enough, Lord. . . . Take my life; I am no better than my ancestors" (1 Kgs. 19:3–4). Even though God had never told Elijah to flee, he still graciously provided for him by sending an angel with freshly baked bread and a jar of water!

God will surely provide for all the needs of the Back to Jerusalem movement if we remain faithful to him and obedient to his leading. The details of how he will do it we leave to him. He might call every rural Christian family in China to dedicate a chicken and its eggs to help fund the Back to Jerusalem workers. If he does, then that would be millions of eggs each month! Or he may choose to provide through overseas believers with a heart for the vision. We do not know; the choice is up to him.

We have noticed that many Christians in the West have an abundance of material possessions, yet they live in a backslidden state. They have silver and gold, but they don't rise up and walk in Jesus' name. In China few of us have any possessions to hold us down, so there's nothing preventing us from moving out for the Lord. The ministry of the Chinese church is like that of Peter at the Beautiful Gate. He told the crippled beggar, *"Silver or gold I do not have, but what I have I give you. In the name of Jesus Christ of Nazareth, walk!"* (Acts 3:6). We can't afford any big programs or fancy gospel presentations. All we have to give people is Jesus.

We are praying that God will use the Chinese church to help the Western church wake up and walk in the power of the Holy Spirit. It's almost impossible for the church in China to go to sleep in its present situation. There's always something to keep us on the run, and it's very difficult to sleep while you're running!

We have seen thousands of times that it does not matter that an evangelist or missionary is poor and uneducated according to the standards of the world. All that matters is whether the hand of God is on that person. *"When a man's ways are pleasing to the Lord, he makes even his enemies live at peace with him"* (Prov. 16:7). God's gifts to a Christian can open remarkable doors and opportunities that result in God being glorified and his kingdom expanded. *"A gift opens the way for the giver and ushers him into the presence of the great"* (Prov. 18:16).

We don't know how the Lord will provide for Back to Jerusalem, but we are determined that our eyes will be focused on the hand of God and not on human hands. We also believe that this vision is very precious to the Lord, and that he will not allow people to participate in it who are not willing to walk in humility and dependence on heaven for their daily bread. *"Cursed is the one who trusts in man, who depends on flesh for his strength and whose heart turns away from the Lord"* (Jer. 17:5).

# An Army of Worms

The Back to Jerusalem mission and the fulfilment of the Great Commission face powerful adversaries. Islam holds more than a billion souls in captivity and blindness. Buddhism and Hinduism have been established for more than two thousand years. The devil feels safe in these strongholds that have largely gone unchallenged throughout Christian history.

When faith-filled believers start taking flames of fire from God's altar into these dark regions, and those fires start spreading to others and the light increases, Satan will be furious. *"Woe to the earth and the sea, because the devil has gone down to you! He is filled with fury, because he knows that his time is short"* (Rev. 12:12).

Satan will not surrender without a bloody fight! But when the devil fights against God's children he is fighting against God himself, and our Lord's weakness is much stronger than the devil's strength. Nevertheless, we expect that much blood will be spilled. One of the most powerful ways we can overcome the spiritual giants of Islam, Buddhism, and Hinduism is by witnessing with our own blood and laying down our lives. For each Christian that the devil tries to kill, the light of the gospel will shine a little brighter and his hold on the people will loosen little by little.

It will not be an army of elephants that marches into nations like Saudi Arabia, Afghanistan, and Iran with the gospel, trampling down the strongholds. Sometimes it seems as if a lot of mission effort consists of "elephant" plans—huge and grandiose strategies for overwhelming the devil's strongholds and making him surrender his captives. But it is easy for border guards to detect an elephant entering the country! It makes a lot of noise and is impossible to hide. Elephants are easy to catch because they move slowly and are so visible. This seems to be how much mission work is conducted today. (Please understand we are talking in generalities here, for we know many of the Lord's people from all around the world have faithfully been laboring in these difficult nations for years. God bless them!)

Instead of an army of elephants, we believe God wants to send an army of insects and crawling creatures to cause the collapse of the house of Buddha, the house of Hinduism, and the house of Mohammed.

The Chinese church is not strong in human terms. We don't have a lot of money or any grandiose plans. But we are an army of little ants, worms, and termites who know how to work underground, because that is how we have learned to work in China for decades. The word of God tells us how we should fight the spiritual fight and offers great encouragement to little creatures like us:

*"Do not be afraid, O worm Jacob, O little Israel, for I myself will help you,"*
*declares the Lord, your Redeemer, the Holy One of Israel. "See, I will make*
*you into a threshing sledge, new and sharp, with many teeth. You will*
*thresh the mountains and crush them, and reduce the hills to chaff. You will*
*winnow them, the wind will pick them up, and a gale will blow them away."*
(Isa. 41:14–16)

While an elephant cannot advance into sensitive areas, little worms and ants can go anywhere. They can go into temples, mosques, and even into king's palaces.

*Four things on earth are small, yet they are extremely wise: Ants are*
*creatures of little strength, yet they store up their food in the summer; conies*
*are creatures of little power, yet they make their home in the crags; locusts*
*have no king, yet they advance together in ranks; a lizard can be caught with*
*the hand, yet it is found in king's palaces.* (Prov. 30:24–28)

This is how the Chinese Christians will operate during the Back to Jerusalem mission. We will not make much noise, but will secretly and quietly do the Lord's work underground. We will be quite difficult to detect. You may not hear many victorious reports of church growth coming back from the Middle East or Southeast Asia, but be assured that our ants, worms, and termites are already there, quietly working away, slowly loosening the foundations of Islam, Buddhism, and Hinduism. You will not see any great or small church buildings resulting from our efforts because we are determined to do what the Lord has led us to do in China these past fifty years and establish spiritual fellowships of believers who meet in their homes. We won't build a single church building anywhere, but the Lord will be building up his church of living stones, with Jesus as the cornerstone.

Termites are very hard to detect. They do their destructive work inside the walls of homes and underneath the floorboards. Usually, the owner of the house has no clue that his magnificent structure is being eaten away until it is too late and it collapses in a heap! The termite can do what even an elephant is unable to do.

There are many Biblical examples of little creatures causing great havoc in the houses of the mighty.

The proud and arrogant Pharaoh refused to let God's people go, so to encourage him to reconsider the Lord did not send a mighty army of angels but a series of plagues including frogs, gnats, and flies. Moses told Pharaoh what God would do:

> *I will plague your whole country with frogs. The Nile will teem with frogs. They will come up into your palace and your bedroom and onto your bed, into the houses of your officials and on your people, and into your ovens and kneading troughs. The frogs will go up on you and your people and all your officials.* (Exod. 8:2–4)

Pharaoh saw no reason to be concerned about his oppressed Israelite slaves and he showed no respect for God. But when these small creatures pestered him in his palace bedroom he took note! Sometimes it is not large initiatives that are the most effective, but the unified efforts of many small pests.

In the second chapter of the Book of Joel, we have a vivid description of an army of locusts that the Lord refers to as *"my great army that I sent among you"* (Joel 2:25). Although Joel refers to the invading Babylonian army of the time, the characteristics of that army are worth emulating. Let's look at why this army of locusts was so effective:

> *At the sight of them, nations are in anguish; every face turns pale.*
> *They charge like warriors; they scale walls like soldiers.*
> *They all march in line, not swerving from their course.*
> *They do not jostle each other; each marches*
>    *straight ahead.*
> *They plunge through defences without breaking ranks.*
> *They rush upon the city, they run along the wall.*
> *They climb into the houses; like thieves they enter through the*
>    *windows . . . .*
> *The Lord thunders at the head of his army; his forces are beyond*
>    *number,*
> *And mighty are those who obey his commands.*
>
> Joel 2:6–9, 11

Ants and termites have a spirit of teamwork. They are so small that they realize they can achieve nothing by themselves, so they work together to achieve their goals, *"they advance together in ranks."* By the time the leaders of these nations realize that an invading army of ants and worms has slipped into their midst, it will be too late to drive them out!

Herod was a king with little regard for God or the people of God. Like the nations of the world, he was proud, pompous, and arrogant, fearing neither God nor man. He was a law unto himself, thinking his authority was final, his reign impregnable. Surely this is how many of the Muslim, Buddhist, and Hindu nations feel today! They are sure that they have the truth, and are so entrenched in their traditions that they are quick to persecute any traces of Christianity and extinguish the slightest sign of spiritual light that the Lord graciously sends their way. How foolish they are! They do not know that Jesus Christ has all power and authority in both heaven and earth! (Matt. 28:18). They think they are completely safe, not realizing that the King of Kings and Lord of Lords will destroy them all with the breath of his mouth. As the prophet Isaiah declared, *"the government will be on his shoulders"* (Isa. 9:6).

Think of what happened to Herod. One day Herod, *"wearing his royal robes, sat down on his throne and delivered a public address to the people. They shouted, 'This is the voice of a god, not of a man'"* (Acts 12: 21–22).

Herod must have felt that things were going great for him at that moment. He had succeeded in making a name for himself, and now the people were shouting his praises. But what Herod didn't realize was that his authority had only been loaned to him by God, and God was about to take it away: *"Immediately, because Herod did not give praise to God, an angel of the Lord struck him down, and he was eaten by worms and died. But the word of God continued to increase and spread"* (Acts 12:23–24).

Herod was dead, but the word of God continued its glorious course, changing the hearts and minds of men and women, boys and girls from every nation, tribe, and language. Nothing can ever defeat the advance of God's word. As Isaiah says, *"The grass withers and the flowers fall, but the word of our God stands forever"* (Isa. 40:8). The psalmist makes the same point: *"Your word, O Lord, is eternal; it stands firm in the heavens"* (Ps. 119:89), and so does Jesus: *"Heaven and earth will pass away, but my words will never pass away"* (Luke 21:33).

As our missionaries take the banner of the Lord into the dark nations, you will probably hear nothing of it. In fact, we are hoping that you won't specifically know what we are doing, for if you do hear about our activities, that means the governments in those lands who seek to keep Christianity beyond their borders will also know what we are doing. It is better if they find out that Jesus has come and taken over their house once it is too late to do anything about it! By God's grace we will be like little worms, ants, and termites, quietly but consistently working away, loosening the foundations of the houses of Buddha, Hinduism, and Mohammed, until they collapse.

# 9

# Answers to Key Questions

*Why is the Chinese church sending missionaries outside China? Shouldn't you be focusing on your own country first?*

Some people have challenged the fact we are sending missionaries outside China. They say we should stay in China and win our own country before we consider sending missionaries out. To this illogical argument we respond with a simple question, "Then why does your country send missionaries? Is everyone in your country saved?"

If we stay home and refuse to advance until we have completely finished the job here, we will never be able to take the gospel to the world. Surely God's way is for us to be winning our home at the same time as we are sending new workers to the ends of the earth! Our vision to reach the world does not mean we will stop or slow down our efforts to reach all of China with the gospel!

The two will take place hand-in-hand.

We believe the best way for the Chinese church to remain strong is to keep it motivated to reach out to the nations of the world. When believers focus on serving the Lord and reaching the lost, God blesses them and the church remains sharp. When we become self-centred and critical of each other, Satan has deceived us and the church becomes a blunt, useless instrument.

*It's clear that house church leaders are completely committed to the Back to Jerusalem vision, but has the vision reached the ordinary believers in China yet?*

We've been working and praying that the vision to complete the Great Commission will become the vision of all believers in China.

We have no problem getting our believers involved in evangelism. Once saved, they have a burning desire to witness and reach the lost. When they read Jesus' words, they have a desire to take the gospel to every nation. The problem has been how to implement strategies that will enable them to move outside our nation as missionaries.

The believers in our churches understand the importance and the responsibility of Back to Jerusalem, but they haven't known what to do about it. You must remember that almost no one in our churches has ever been outside China, so simply thinking about how to get there has been a major step. But gradually, over the last several years, the Back to Jerusalem movement has gathered momentum among the Christians in China, until today the pressure has built so strong that more of the church must be sent outside China soon. They must let some steam off before they explode!

In 2000 many house church leaders left China and attended a Back to Jerusalem meeting in a Southeast Asian country. For almost all of us, it was the first time we had left China. The country where our meetings were held is a Buddhist stronghold, where the overwhelming majority of people don't know Christ.

This trip had a deep effect on us as we saw hundreds of temples, multitudes of lost souls worshipping idols, young boys proudly walking down the roads as trainee monks, and a complete absence of gospel light everywhere we traveled. In China, of course, there is still tremendous spiritual darkness in many places and there are areas where Buddhism is strong, but there is nothing as concentrated as what we saw all over that nation.

We all returned to China changed people. Now that we had seen the need with our eyes and felt it with our hearts, missions ceased to be a theoretical concern and became a stark reality in our lives and ministries. We all returned to our churches with a new urgency and burden for Back to Jerusalem.

We are praying with tears in our eyes for ways to get our churches involved more directly in the Back to Jerusalem vision. We are training our leaders inside China in meetings where we share the vision. They then take the vision back to their house churches. Materials are being produced to help people gain a better understanding, and we are seeing more and more Christians with a burden for worldwide mission.

God is also directly calling ordinary people to serve him as missionaries in certain countries or among specific ethnic groups. Here is one of many similar testimonies of how this is taking place: A sister received a dream from the Lord in which she heard the word *Tamang* and saw herself preaching the gospel to a group of tribal people. She has no idea what this word meant, and prayed earnestly for the Lord to reveal more. About two years later she was given a small prayer booklet that contained information about the unreached people groups of Nepal. She wept as she read about the Tamang people, a Buddhist tribe in that country! The Tamang people shown in a picture in the booklet had exactly the same physical features and dress as she had seen in her dream. She has now gone to Nepal as a missionary to the Tamang people.

*Where did the Chinese church get the figure of 100,000 missionaries to be sent outside China? Is it a real number, or just an indication that you would like to send a large number of missionaries?*

Christians need to understand that this number is not some fixed numerical goal that we have. It is merely an indication of the *minimum* number of missionaries we plan to send out. This number was first arrived at when many leaders of different house church networks met together to pray and discuss Back to Jerusalem. At the time we estimated that together we had approximately one million 'full-time' Christian workers in our churches. We believe the very least we should do is give a tithe of these leaders to foreign missions. That is how we first arrived at the figure of 100,000.

We have noticed that many Westerners tend to be very excited and motivated by numbers, but we are not. Our goal is not to send 100,000 missionaries out of China. Our goal is nothing less than the completion of the Great Commission so that the Lord Jesus Christ will return for his bride, to bring all of human history to the moment in Scripture where voices are heard in heaven, proclaiming, *"The kingdom of the world has become the kingdom of our Lord and of his Christ, and he will reign for ever and ever"* (Rev. 11:15).

That is our goal and purpose! We are willing to do whatever it takes to fulfil this vision and be obedient to the calling.

If it takes more than 100,000 workers, then there will be more workers; if it takes fewer, there will be fewer. More than likely, the figure of 100,000 is a conservative estimate. We are concentrating on getting the job done in the power of the Lord. The details of *how* this happens we leave to the Lord.

When we were selecting the first group of Back to Jerusalem missionaries, it was actually difficult to keep the numbers down to just thirty-nine. House church leaders shared the vision for Back to Jerusalem in just a few meetings, and immediately people jumped up with their arms raised, proclaiming, "I will go! I am willing to go and die for Jesus!" In some meetings over half of the people in attendance insisted on being among the first Back to Jerusalem workers, and in the end we had to insist that only thirty-nine would go. We told the others to wait for the next opportunity.

The Back to Jerusalem missionaries will not all be believers from Mainland China either. There are tens of millions of Chinese people living in overseas countries, many of whom are Christians. Thousands of them are also receiving a call from God to give their lives to the Back to Jerusalem vision.

In February 2003, hundreds of Chinese pastors, leaders and lay workers from ten different nations in Europe gathered in Paris for the first Bringing the Gospel Back to Jerusalem Conference. Brother Yun was the keynote speaker.

From the very beginning, the Holy Spirit was moving in a mighty way in these meetings. Every night, hundreds of people came forward for prayer. The direction of many lives was completely changed, and many were empowered by the Holy Spirit in a new, fresh way. Brother Yun's message was simple. He emphasized God's call to the Chinese people to "get the job done" and to bring the gospel into unevangelized areas between China and Jerusalem. Again and again, young people with tears in their eyes rushed forward for prayer and committed their lives to spreading the good news, willing to do whatever God is asking of them.

Altogether, more than five hundred people made the decision to commit their lives to the Lord of this mission and are now waiting for further instructions as to when and where to go. Some of the leaders shared how God had spoken to them when they were still living in China, how he had challenged them to leave China and move to Europe in order to stir up the Western church—especially the young people—and to join hands with them in bringing the gospel to the most unreached parts of the world. During this meeting they praised God for the revelation of his plan for the Back to Jerusalem vision. Many similar meetings are planned for other European cities and other parts of the world.

God is truly doing something amazing, and thousands of new

Back to Jerusalem missionaries are already being called to action by the Lord of the harvest.

*When thousands of Back to Jerusalem workers leave China and go all over the 10/40 window, do you have any plans to keep track of them?*

Of course! These structures are being put in place right now. We realize that our workers will need spiritual and physical assistance. They will need pastoral care to give them spiritual encouragement and keep them walking closely with the Lord.

Because the Back to Jerusalem vision is a call to the whole church, there will obviously be many different workers from different backgrounds going out for the Lord. However, as far as the ones coming from our church networks are concerned, we certainly do plan to keep track of them and do everything possible to help them as they complete the Great Commission. There will be (and already are) other Chinese missionaries going out to the nations who are not linked to our fellowships. We pray a great blessing from the Lord on all people who call on the name of the Lord and who desire to make his name known.

We also believe that some missionaries will need to return to China from time to time to report to the church what God is doing through them. We have found this to be extremely important in our house churches. It encourages the sending believers and helps mobilize new workers for the vision.

Certain locations will serve as key centers for the training and administration of Back to Jerusalem workers. Plans are already under way for a secure headquarters for the movement and for prayer and information centers where there will be continual intercession, asking the Lord to bless the work and remove all demonic hindrances.

*What about security? What plans do you have to protect Back to Jerusalem workers?*

Many Western missionary organizations pull their workers out of a place as soon as there is any sign of trouble. Advance will be very slow with such a mentality! If self-preservation is that important, then there is no point in going in the first place. God looks for children who are willing to die for him if necessary. The countries in the Back to Jerusalem vision do not welcome the gospel and there will certainly be trouble when anyone attempts to take it to them.

All the way through the Bible there was trouble when God's people proclaimed the truth. Elijah was called the *"troubler of Israel"* (1 Kgs. 18:17). When Paul and Silas appeared before the authorities in Philippi, their accusers said they were *"throwing our city into an uproar"* (Acts 16:20). As you read through the Book of Acts, it seems that every time Paul preached the gospel there was one of two reactions: revival or riot!

We understand that there is a time for caution and a time to escape. There is biblical precedent for this too, for the Apostle Paul was placed in a basket and lowered over the Damascus city wall to escape those who wished to kill him (see Acts 9:22–25).

But there is also a time when Christians should march forward regardless of danger. Consider the courageous words of the Apostle Paul:

> And now, compelled by the Spirit, I am going to Jerusalem, not knowing what will happen to me there. I only know that in every city the Holy Spirit warns me that prison and hardships are facing me. However, I consider my life worth nothing to me, if only I may finish the race and complete the task the Lord Jesus has given me—the task of testifying to the gospel of God's grace. (Acts 20:22–24)

Any believer who truly wants to obey God will make trouble. Someone who merely wants to avoid conflict and maintain the status quo will not achieve much for the Lord. The structures that keep countless millions of people enslaved to sin and Satan must be confronted before they will crumble, and when you confront evil there will always be trouble.

This is the main reason house church Christians in China have been persecuted for decades. They are not persecuted just because of their faith in God. If they chose, they could all settle down in a government-controlled Three-Self church, worship God each Sunday, and live relatively stress free lives as long as they keep their beliefs to themselves and don't try to share them with others.

The reason house church Christians are arrested and imprisoned in China is because they cannot keep quiet. They cannot possibly keep their mouths shut because Jesus has revealed himself to them and they have been radically changed from the inside out. They understand how the prophet Jeremiah felt when he said, *"If I say, 'I will not mention him or speak any more in his name,' his word is in my heart like a fire, a fire shut up in my bones. I am weary of holding it in; indeed, I cannot"* (Jer. 20:9).

Western Christians often ask us why there is persecution in China and other countries and not in the West. There are several possible responses to this question, but we would like to start by asking one question in return: "Do you boldly preach the truth of God's word to sinners inside and outside your churches?" If you do, you will soon find out that there is persecution wherever you are.

Scripture says that *"those who desire to live a godly life in Christ Jesus will be persecuted"* (2 Tim. 3:12). It does not say that they "may" be persecuted, but that they "will" be persecuted. If you are not being persecuted, the problem isn't with God's word. Perhaps the question to be asked is "Are you truly desiring to live a godly life in Christ Jesus?" Persecution may take different forms from one country to another, but there will be persecution.

As the Back to Jerusalem vision unfolds, we know that *"a righteous man may have many troubles, but the Lord delivers him from them all; he protects all his bones; not one of them will be broken"* (Ps. 34:19–20).

The Muslim and Buddhist nations can torture us, imprison us, and starve us, but they can do no more than we have already experienced in China for many decades. Thousands of young men and women will go as missionaries who are not afraid to die for Jesus. They are not afraid to bleed, for they know their bodies are merely temporary tents to be used in the Lord's service and that one day they will be in paradise where there is no pain and no tears. They are not only ready to die for the gospel, they are expecting it.

*Have the house churches experienced much success reaching Muslims and Buddhists inside China? If not, why do you think you will succeed outside China?*

The Chinese house churches have only really started to obey God's call to win the minorities in China in the last few years. There were evangelists trying to reach minorities before then, but most house church work was targeted to Han Chinese communities.

It was only when a Western brother came and taught the house church leaders that there are more than 400 unreached minority groups in our own country that we began to pray and target them more seriously. God gave us a great burden for their evangelization, and hundreds of new teams have either already gone or are currently in preparation for ministry to the minorities of China.

We have already started to receive good reports from some parts of southern Xinjiang, where God has used house church workers to win many Muslims to Christ after God has confirmed the preaching of the word with miracles.

Some people say that the Muslims in China hate the Han Chinese so much that we can never lead them to Christ, but God is proving that this idea is wrong. If we go to them in true humility and in the power of God, they see that we are different and many Muslims come to Jesus.

The Tibetans and other strong Buddhist groups are in a sense even more difficult to reach with the gospel than Muslims because Buddhists have absolutely no concept of a Creator God or of personal sin. Yet we have many evangelists working among Tibetans. Just in Lhasa City alone, the capital of Tibet, we have almost a hundred house church evangelists reaching out. While it is true that not many Tibetans have believed, a few small Tibetan fellowships have been established, and God is teaching our workers how to pray and work more effectively. They have learned that strategies used in other parts of China will not necessarily work in Tibet, so they are seeking God for revelation about how to win the Tibetans. When God gives the key, the door will open!

Certainly, as far as Chinese Buddhists are concerned, we have seen many thousands believe in the Lord throughout China. Some of our key house church leaders today were formerly Buddhist monks who came to faith in Christ and experienced his life-transforming power.

We don't consider reaching the minorities of China to be a separate vision; this is part of the Back to Jerusalem vision. The lessons our workers learn in reaching Muslims and Buddhists within China's borders will prove valuable as we reach Muslims and Buddhists outside China.

## Do you think miracles will be an important factor in reaching the nations?

Miracles are not something we should seek after in themselves. They are not a toy for us to play with but an integral part of the gospel. We are not called to follow miracles, but the Bible says signs and wonders will follow us when we preach the gospel (see Mark 16:17–20). The miracles act as evidence that the message is true. When we tell people that Jesus is alive, and they see him heal a cripple or deliver a demon-possessed person, they will easily believe the message!

In China's house churches we estimate that as many as 80 percent of believers first come to Jesus because they receive a miraculous healing or deliverance from the Lord. They give their lives unreservedly to God in response.

The Scriptures point out that when new believers both hear the gospel and see a demonstration of its power, their faith will be deep. That is why the Apostle Paul wrote, *"My message and my preaching were not with wise and persuasive words, but with a demonstration of the Spirit's power, so that your faith might not rest on man's wisdom, but on God's power"* (1 Cor. 2:4). It is much better for faith to rest on God's power than on human wisdom!

In China new believers are often willing to endure tremendous hardship, torture and harassment, even when they have believed in Christ for just a few weeks or months. When someone comes to Jesus because they have experienced his power operating in their lives, they have no trouble in believing he is alive, because they have already met him! If they were ever to deny Christ, they would not only have to reject God's word, but also their own experiences.

Thus miracles are an important factor, but they are not something we seek in themselves. They follow automatically when the good news is preached to the lost. We should not follow miracles, but miracles should follow us when we preach! This has been our experience all over China.

## What are the biggest concerns you have about things that might stop or slow down the Back to Jerusalem vision?

Spiritual elders and intercessors in the house churches are somewhat concerned that the spiritual life of the present generation of believers is not as strong as in previous years. China is becoming economically affluent and there are opportunities and temptations for young Christians today that didn't exist fifteen or twenty years ago. The lure of the world is stronger than in the past. Young men and women who desire to live wholeheartedly for Jesus and the advance of the gospel face a struggle to maintain this focus.

When we brought our concerns before the Lord in prayer, he clearly showed us that the house churches of China will remain in revival as long as they remain obedient to the vision to preach the gospel back to Jerusalem. If we lose our first love and start to focus on our own needs, our spiritual life will shrivel up and die. As long as we strive to obey God's call to take the gospel to the Muslim, Buddhist, and Hindu nations, he will bless our churches and revival in China will continue. This principle is not only a spiritual one, but is true in nature also. A flower or plant that looks upward and outward flourishes and reflects the beauty of the Creator, but one that turns inward soon dies and its true beauty is never revealed to the world.

We encourage Christians and churches around the world not to focus on their own needs and desires! If you do, you will surely shrivel up and die. God's principle is that when you seek to bring blessing to others, your own lives will be blessed. When you make missionary outreach to nations that have never heard about Jesus the priority of your church, you will not fail to be blessed and revived: *"Seek first his kingdom and his righteousness, and all of these things will be given to you as well"* (Matt. 6:33).

Christians or churches that seek blessings for their own pleasure and enjoyment are in danger of idolatry. Jesus said, *"He who speaks on his own does so to gain honor for himself, but he who works for the honor of the one who sent him is a man of truth; there is nothing false about him"* (John 7:18).

So many Christians are doing their own thing, and don't know or even seem to care that God's cloud and pillar of fire have moved on! Let's decide to wake up and find out what the Lord is doing and see how we can get involved! The difference between mere "Christian activity" and being a front-line soldier in the Lord's battle is as wide as day and night.

When you are truly obeying the Lord's call you please God, and when you are in step with the work of the Holy Spirit you begin to feel the heartbeat of our loving Savior. Your work stops being a chore and starts becoming a natural overflow of the love of God that has been deposited in your heart.

If the Chinese church settles down and stops preaching the gospel, then the fire of God that has been among us for so long with surely die down, but as long as we are true to our call, it will be impossible for the fire to die down! If a man picks a hot stick out of a fire and runs with it, the movement will fan the flame back into life. If he sits down and watches it long enough, the fire will diminish and finally be snuffed out altogether. The Christian life is one of action for Jesus, not inaction.

As more of our missionaries go to the nations with the fire of Jesus Christ in their hearts and a two-edged sword, the word of God, in their hands, the believers back home in China will need to be praying for them every day. As reports come back of people being brought to salvation, and of persecution and martyrdom, the church in China will find their own zeal and commitment fanned into flame. We have seen this many times in our house churches. We send evangelists to all four corners of China, and when they come back months later and share how the Lord has used them, with testimonies of miracles and breakthroughs, their home churches are encouraged and challenged to win more souls and live more radically for Jesus.

*Do you have a timeline for when you expect the Back to Jerusalem movement to be operating at full speed?*

It has already begun, and is gathering momentum with each day! We do not have our own timeline; we just want to obey God's will and leave the timing to him.

The important thing for the Chinese church is that we are determined not to fall short of what God wants to do through us in this generation. We don't want to be judged because we only did half, or even 80 percent of what God wanted us to do. We want to be found 100 percent faithful! When the work doesn't get done, it is never God's fault. His will is not unsearchable, and he says, *"Surely, as I have planned, so it will be, and as I have purposed, so it will stand"* (Isa. 14:24). Our prayer is that we will not miss the mark and leave the job undone. We pray we will be like King David: *"For when David had served God's purpose in his own generation, he fell asleep"* (Acts 13:36).

We have already seen how many important things have started

lining up in ways that are making the Back to Jerusalem vision a present reality. For example, until recently the Chinese government allowed very few of its citizens to travel abroad. This created a deep desire in people to go and see what the rest of the world is like. There is a tremendous hunger to learn about other countries, their people and cultures. The same applies to the church in China. In recent years the travel restrictions have been gradually eased and now it is much easier for Chinese to get passports and travel abroad. The easing of restrictions will surely only continue in the future. We believe this is part of God's sovereign plan to facilitate the Back to Jerusalem vision.

We believe the Chinese church can succeed in bringing down the religious giants of Islam, Buddhism, and Hinduism because the Lord has taught us how to work in a nation where there is great opposition to the advance of the gospel. Much effort has been put into evangelizing some of the countries in the Middle East, but without much fruit. These nations are vigilantly on guard against Christianity coming from America. They have sealed their front doors as tightly as they can against Christianity, and they closely monitor every activity of Westerners who come to their country. While they spend all their energy guarding their front doors, the Chinese Christians may be able to quietly slip in the back door with the gospel!

The Lord has been training the Chinese house churches for the past fifty years through imprisonment, torture, suffering, and hardship. Thousands have been treated brutally in prison; thousands more have been sent out across the country as evangelists with nobody to rely on except God himself. They have seen numerous miracles and have come to a deep trust in Jesus that could not have been learned in any other way than through hardship and suffering. We are not saying we are any better than anyone else! That is not the issue. But we do believe the Lord has put the Chinese church through these experiences to train us to complete this specific task of taking the gospel back to Jerusalem. We have become soldiers of steel, tempered in the furnace of affliction. We do not fear what people can do to us.

Before the American and British forces invaded Iraq, the Iraqis boldly proclaimed their willingness to die for their cause, but as soon as the fighting began their army melted away, offering no resistance at all. By contrast, the Back to Jerusalem army will be a humble one that advances on its knees, every day and every minute acknowledging that without God's help and the power of the Holy Spirit, there can be no successful outcome for the kingdom of God. God is the one who will direct the course of this battle. *"Unless the Lord builds the house, its builders labor in vain"* (Ps. 127:1)

## As the Chinese missionaries spread out across the 10/40 window, do they plan to work with local Christians in each country?

This question is somewhat irrelevant because the aim of Back to Jerusalem is to share Christ in places and among people groups where there is no gospel witness. If there is no gospel, then by definition there will be no other Christians working in that place. Our attitude is that of the Apostle Paul, who said, *"It has always been my ambition to preach the gospel where Christ was not known, so that I would not be building on someone else's foundation"* (Rom. 15:20). When we enter a particular country, our desire will be to find out where the neediest places are, where there are no Christians, and to work there. We don't want to get bogged down trying to light a new fire where others are already burning. We want to go to the darkest, blackest regions where the light has never been seen before.

We are, however, aware that small numbers of Christians do exist even in countries like Saudi Arabia, Afghanistan and Iran. Our intention is not to just "do our own thing" without consulting the existing body of Christ. As the Lord leads, we want to partner and work hand in hand with Thai, Indian, and Arab Christians, or those from any other group, if the result will be to see God's kingdom advance more quickly. We welcome true partnership. We need local believers to teach us their language and culture and many other things that will help us be more effective. We may be able to share some of the fire and vision that the Lord has given us in China with the local churches.

Therefore, we will try to work in cooperation with local believers as far as possible, but if our ministry aims are totally different from theirs, it may be necessary for us to respectfully agree to work separately.

We have several key principles that we believe God has taught us and which we plan to take into the mission field. For example, we refuse to be drawn into the spirit of denominationalism in any way. We are going to preach the gospel and see sinners come to the feet of Jesus and experience the new life that he won for them on the cross. We don't want any part in promoting any denomination. We only want to promote Jesus and ask the Holy Spirit to confirm whether Jesus is alive or not. Nowhere in God's word does it say that if we lift up our church or methods or doctrine, the Holy Spirit will bless us and bring revival. But Jesus clearly told us who we should lift up: *"But I, when I am lifted up from the earth, will draw all men to myself"* (John 12:32).

We are also not interested in erecting any church buildings. We don't believe the world needs another single church building. They need Jesus, and they need to worship and grow in God's grace with other believers within their own homes, according to the pattern of the first church in the New Testament (see, for example, Acts 5:42, 20:20, Rom. 16:5.)

Although we do have some strong convictions about how God's work should be done, let us reiterate that even if our methods are different from those of other Christians, we will still strive to honor and have fellowship with all believers who have been bought by the precious blood of Jesus Christ.

### How will you know if the Back to Jerusalem movement has been successful? How will you know when you have achieved your goals?

This is an interesting question, and after thinking about it, we have come to realize we are called to nothing less than the evangelization of all the remaining unreached peoples—more than five thousand of them! According to the Bible, the blood of Jesus has *"purchased men for God from every tribe and language and people and nation"* (Rev. 5:9). When the Lord helps us to achieve our goals, what will have been accomplished is nothing less than the fulfilment of the Great Commission!

Many people want to know when the end of the world will come. Some people talk about wars and natural disasters, others about global catastrophes. Many say you should watch what happens in Israel, because Israel holds the key. We think it would be better to pay attention to the words of Jesus, because he was asked the very same question by his disciples, *"What will be the sign of your coming and the end of the age?"* (Matt. 24:3).

Jesus didn't ignore the question, but first he mentioned a number of things that would happen before his Second Coming and the end of the age. He spoke about false prophets, about rumors of wars, about earthquakes, and about persecution of believers. *"Such things must happen, but the end is still to come."* (Matt. 24:6).

What, then, was the final sign that would take place before Jesus' return? He clearly told his disciples, *"And this gospel of the kingdom will be preached in the whole world as a testimony to all nations, and then the end will come"* (Matt. 24:14). The Greek word translated "nations" in this verse does not mean political countries but ethnic groups. The plan of God is to give a clear witness about his Son to every branch of humanity, and once that happens the end will come.

How will we know when we have achieved our goals? We will know because Jesus will have returned and the end will have come! Until that time, we plan to keep preaching the good news to every person who has yet to hear it.

## Who can be involved in Back to Jerusalem?

The task of completing the Great Commission is not only for the Chinese church! It may sound like that as you read this book because we have been talking about the specific history, vision, and strategies that God has given the churches of China in regard to one particular aspect of this plan. But the vision of taking the gospel Back to Jerusalem and fulfilling the Great Commission was given by Jesus two thousand years ago to Christians of all generations, from all nations. The invitation is open to all people who have been born again by the Spirit of God and burdened for the salvation of mankind.

We know there are many thousands of wonderful, loving Christians from all kinds of countries who are already reaching out to the lost in Muslim, Buddhist, and Hindu nations, and we pray for them every day and thank God for their ministries!

Scripture offers encouragement to all people irrespective of nationality or background. Jesus said, *"I say to you that many will*

*come from the east and the west, and will take their places at the feast with*
*Abraham, Isaac and Jacob in the kingdom of heaven"* (Matt. 8:11).

Not only is salvation offered to all people of all races and ethnic
divisions, but Jesus' command that his disciples take the gospel to
the ends of the earth is given to all Christians. Some Christians seem
to have got the idea that "missions" is "the West to the Rest". But
nowhere in the Bible does it say that missionaries have to be white!
They don't need to come from wealthy countries, nor do they need to
have graduated from a Bible school or seminary. A missionary only
needs to be someone who loves the Lord Jesus and has a passion
to reach the lost world for him. That is the only qualification for
missionary service. Mark 16:15, which contains the command to *"go
into all the world and preach the good news to all creation,"* is not only
part of the English and Chinese Bibles, but of every Bible in every
language into which the word of God has been translated. Christians
in Africa, Europe, South America, and Asia all have the same
command from Jesus. Regardless of their social, political, racial, or
economic circumstances, they are to take the good news to the ends
of the earth. All Christians who read God's command will one day be
held accountable for what they did about it.

There have been times when God has given Christians in
other parts of Asia a clear call and strategy for world missions. For
example, the churches of Nagaland in Northeast India experienced
tremendous revival in the 1950s, 60s, and 70s. Today practically all
Naga people profess faith in Jesus Christ. In the early 1970s the Nagas
made a commitment to send 10,000 cross-cultural missionaries
throughout the 10/40 window. We would like to encourage the
Nagas, and believers everywhere, to renew their commitment to
God and the Great Commission. Back to Jerusalem truly belongs
to the worldwide church. We hope that this vision will inspire you
to look at your own life and have the same call and commitment to
reaching the lost. We will never achieve our goal unless we all pray
and work together.

Who then can be involved in the Back to Jerusalem movement?
All whom the Lord calls, and who are willing to start by living the
Back to Jerusalem life wherever they are.

What does this mean? It means that if you are willing to spill your
blood and die for the vision, you are truly a partner of the Chinese

church as we march on the strongholds of Islam, Buddhism, and Hinduism

## Do all Christians believe in the Back to Jerusalem vision?

As we have presented the Back to Jerusalem vision to church leaders around the world, we have seen that some strongly sense it is a vision given by God. They can see God's hand in it and are eager to be involved in any way they can. Other Christians, however, cannot grasp the vision even after hearing about it several times. Even some Western mission leaders have been unable to see any value in it—"utter foolishness" is how some described the vision. They are like those spoken of by the prophet Isaiah: *"The Lord has brought over you a deep sleep. He has sealed your eyes . . . he has covered your heads . . . For you this whole vision is nothing but words sealed in a scroll"* (Isa. 29:10–11).

We are not overly worried about people's responses. We know that God has given us this vision and has gradually unfolded it over the past seventy years. If the vision were not from God it would never have survived the decades of fierce opposition. Many people have already died for this vision. As we present Back to Jerusalem some will understand, while others won't. What matters most is that those whom the Lord calls can clearly discern God's heart and desires. We must be able to walk in the light. It is very dangerous if the church is walking in darkness. If we are in the light and can see clearly, it doesn't matter how many obstacles and difficulties await us on the road ahead, we will be able to clearly see and avoid them. But if the vision is cloudy and visibility is poor, we will never be able to advance as the Lord desires.

You may have seen the vision God has given to take the gospel back to Jerusalem, but if others do not understand what you are talking about, you can rejoice that you are in good company. Whenever people proclaim a vision from the Lord, there is opposition and jealousy. The devil doesn't care if you have your own plan or vision. But when there is a vision that comes from the throne of God, there will be fierce opposition. After all, having a God-given vision does not mean everything will flow smoothly. Joseph received a vision, but when he proclaimed it to his brothers they tried to kill him! He spent many years in prison where the vision must have seemed very distant, but God does not lie. His visions always come to pass if we are patient and obedient. Joseph was eventually released from the dungeon and became the second-in-command in Egypt. Many pastors in China have received a vision from the Lord, only to spend many years in prison before the Lord has fulfilled what he had shown.

If God has given you a vision for his glory, then step out in obedience to the heavenly call. The road may not be easy, but you will succeed if you endure to the very end. In China we sometimes say, "Let's rush to the front line one more time for our King and Christ will come! We can have a holiday for 1,000 years when it is all finished!"

We are thankful that there are many people who understand what this vision is about and want to be involved, even to the point of being willing to die for it! We want to partner with those around the world whom God has elected to join hands with us.

## *How can Christians best pray for Back to Jerusalem?*

- Pray that the fire and zeal to preach the gospel will be ever present in the lives of Chinese Christians.

- Pray that believers' lives will reflect the character and integrity of our Lord.

- Pray that the church will know God's heart and his will so that we will be willing to obey the calling to take the gospel back to Jerusalem and usher in the Second Coming of Christ.

- Pray that those who are called by the name of Jesus will have true unity in the faith. Ask God to break down the man-made walls between us so that we can fulfil this great vision God has given us.

- Pray that believers everywhere in the world will work and pray together to fulfil the Great Commission.

# 10

# Disciples or Just Believers?

*Anyone who does not carry his cross and follow me cannot be my disciple . . . Any of you who does not give up everything he has cannot be my disciple.*

— *Luke 14:27,33*

*From this time many of his disciples turned back and no longer followed him.*

— *John 6:66*

In the next three chapters we would like to share some important principles for God's people around the world if the Back to Jerusalem vision is to be fulfilled. Our prayer is that the Lord will bless you and make you a soldier fit to participate in the completion of the Great Commission.

\*   \*   \*

There are more than two billion professing Christians in the world today. Think about that: two thousand million people who say they follow Jesus Christ! That is a staggering number.

So why then are there still so many needy countries and areas of spiritual darkness in the world today? Why is there still a need for the Back to Jerusalem vision after twenty centuries of Christianity?

The problem lies in the kind of Christianity practised by the majority of believers today. For countless millions of people, following Jesus is little more than a cultural experience. Joining a church means little more than joining a social club where they can meet new people and exchange pleasantries about inconsequential matters. If the Bible is read at all, it is from a sense of duty rather than as part of a relationship with its real, vibrant, and life-changing author.

Jesus is viewed as a historical figure who died on the cross, and as a future figure who will one day come again, but few Christians really, genuinely, walk with Jesus today, sharing their dreams, fears, and concerns with him as a lover, friend, and Lord.

Millions of churches around the world, including inside China, are bound by legalism. Obeying man-made rules has become more important than taking the hand of Jesus and walking with him in the cool of the evening. The Christian life has become an endurance test, and all traces of life and joy have long since evaporated!

Brothers and sisters, don't be deceived, such a bound church is nothing less than a work of Satan, and such a collection of believers will never be able to save any souls for the kingdom of God. It is absolutely impossible for a legalistic believer to lead a single person to Jesus Christ. They may occasionally lead someone else to obey the same rules they do, but they will never lead a thirsty soul to the well of eternal life. How can a person show a lost soul the way to someone they themselves cannot recognize?

One thing is certain: the two billion Muslims, Buddhists, and Hindus we are targeting in the Back to Jerusalem vision will never be reached by passionless Christians. They will only respond when they are confronted by the truth of God's Word as revealed in the lives of true disciples of Jesus who have given up all they have to follow him.

There are more than enough Christian "believers" in the world today. God wants more disciples!

As this book was going to print the deadly SARS virus was spreading across China and parts of Asia. Scientists believe the epidemic is spread by "super-carriers." These super-carriers can infect hundreds of people just by interacting with them. Everywhere they go they spread the virus and people's lives are changed for ever. Christians leaders should be super-carriers of a heavenly virus that only infects the dead—people who are dead to selfish ambitions and human acclaim, whose only desire is to live for God's glory and see his kingdom prosper.[40] Unfortunately the Western church seems to contain a kind of religious anti-virus that seeks to smother and destroy vision-filled super-carriers of the gospel virus. Tens of thousands of churches have become smugly sermon-proof. *"The Lord says: 'These people come near to me with their mouth and honour me with their lips, but their hearts are far from me. Their worship of me is made up only of rules taught by men'"* (Isa. 29:13).

Christians are called to exercise *"faith, hope, and love"* (1 Cor. 13:13), but for millions of churchgoers in congregations affected by an anti-virus, faith has been replaced by hopelessness, hope has succumbed to disillusionment, and love has been swallowed up by cynicism and fear. If you are a believer who feels trapped in despondency and failure, there is hope! But the only way to live the life God has planned for you is to repent, call out to God from your heart, and ask him to give you a vision from heaven that will result in many lives being blessed.

God is looking for super-carriers of the gospel! He wants men and women, boys and girls who are willing to take the fire and love of God to millions of people who will be infected with spiritual life!

Only disciples of Jesus can ever hope to impact the nations for God.

Prior to the 1950s, most Christians in China were also mere "believers" in Christ, and when the heat of affliction came on, many fell away from the faith. Many others, however, got serious about God and decided to follow him whatever the cost. They were gradually transformed into disciples of the Lord Jesus Christ, who not only preached Jesus on the cross but realized that there is also a personal cross on which each disciple will experience crucifixion and pain.

Today most Christians in China's house churches are fully committed disciples of Jesus Christ. Every Christian is a soul-winner; every believer is involved in fulfilling the Great Commission. The work of the church is not done by a few "qualified" individuals but by millions of passionate farmers, office workers, and salesmen and women all over the nation. Some of the greatest evangelists are teenagers who have been called by God to travel from village to village sharing the good news not only about what Jesus has done in the past, but what he can do in the lives of all who surrender to him today.

True disciples are usually people that few understand. They are viewed as potentially unstable fanatics. Often the same governments that tolerate the existence of mere believers will stop at no ends to completely eradicate any disciples within their borders.

Believers try to follow God, but their prayers and commitment are clouded by indecisiveness. Their prayers go like this: "Oh Lord, I am so weak. Please send your power. I am weighed down with sin. Please come and relieve me." If they ever hear the King's call to go somewhere and do something for the sake of his kingdom, they feel they need extra encouragement before they can safely step out:"First let me check with my wife, my pastor, my boss, and my mother-in-law to see if it's OK with them."

A believer always seeks assurances that nothing will go wrong if they step out for Jesus. Only when they are convinced that the coast is clear and no harm will befall them are they willing to take their first step!

Disciples have a different attitude. In China many disciples beg God to give them just a little of his dynamite power. They pray, "Oh God, if you will lend me just a little spiritual dynamite, I promise I will take it to the darkest area I can find, place it there, and pray you will send your fire from heaven to explode it."

God always does.

This is how the Gospel has spread so quickly in China.

*   *   *

There are literally thousands of testimonies we could share with you about disciples in the Chinese church whom God has used in a mighty way. For now, let us share just three testimonies that display different aspects of the life of a true disciple of Jesus.

# The Obedience of Sister Chang

*The reason I wrote to you was to see if you would stand the test and be obedient in everything.*

*— 2 Corinthians 2:9*

When God spoke to Sister Chang, a house church leader from Henan, he told her to do something that made no earthly sense at all. He told her to go and preach the gospel on the steps outside the local police station. Such an action may lead to arrest even in Western nations, and in Communist China it is a sure way to invite severe punishment. But the more Sister Chang prayed about it, the more clearly the inner voice of God continued to tell her to do it. Finally, she saw no option but to obey God.

Standing on the top step outside the police station, she boldly proclaimed the gospel to astonished onlookers. Within a few minutes several officers dragged her inside and placed her under arrest. To the human eye her obedience looked foolish, but God can see things that we can't.

Sister Chang was sentenced without a trial and sent to the local women's prison, where she was placed alongside thousands of spiritually lost souls. She boldly and lovingly proclaimed the gospel to her fellow prisoners. The light of the gospel spread like wildfire. Within just three months, eight hundred women believed in Jesus! The entire atmosphere of the prison changed, and new sounds of praise and worship were heard echoing down the prison hallways and in the courtyard.

The prison director was greatly impressed at the change in the atmosphere and was able to trace it to the preaching of Sister Chang. He brought her into his office and said, "You have made my job easy! There is no more fighting between the prisoners and the women have become gentle and obedient. We need more people like you working here. From today, we have decided to let you go free. We want to give you a full-time job here in the prison, and we will pay you three thousand yuan per month" (about $375 US, a fortune in rural Henan). He continued, "We will also give you a car and your own driver, and will find you comfortable housing."

Sister Chang briefly considered the offer, and then replied, "Twenty years ago I became a disciple of Jesus Christ and he has been wonderful to me. I don't believe your offer of a car, driver, and salary is in line with what Jesus wants to do with my life, and I belong to him. All I want to do is preach the good news."

Despite her rejection of his offer, the director released her from prison that day, and she continued her ministry for the Lord.

It always pays to do what the Lord tells us to do. Don't argue, don't fight it, and don't try to work out all the details with your mind. Just do it. That is one mark of a true disciple of Jesus Christ.

# Sister Yuen of Shanghai

*If anyone comes to me and does not hate his father and mother, his wife and children, his brothers and sisters—yes, even his own life—he cannot be my disciple.*

*— Luke 14:26*

Sister Yuen came from one of the wealthiest families in Shanghai.

In 1967 she was arrested and sent to prison. At the time she was a widow with two young children, a son aged eleven and a daughter aged nine.

After Sister Yuen had been a year in prison her mother—who had been taking care of the children—died. The authorities decided to have "compassion" on her so she could go home and take care of her children. They told her that all she had to do was produce a written confession of her "crimes" and they would free her. They said, "This past year your conduct has been excellent, so now we plan to reward you."

The officials arranged for her small children to be brought to the prison gates for a visit. Yuen was ordered to pack her bags as if she was going home. As soon as she caught a glimpse of her precious children, her heart was torn and tears of love welled up in her eyes.

Then the guards asked her, "What do you want, your Jesus or your children? If you want Jesus you will remain in this prison. If you want your children, you can go home. Surely your God would want you to be kind to your own flesh and blood?"

Sister Yuen's son and daughter called out "Mummy, we miss you! Please come home!"

A prison guard gave Sister Yuen a pencil and a piece of paper and asked her to write down her confession. She wrote in large characters, "Jesus can never be replaced. Even my own children cannot replace Jesus."

She chose to stay in prison.

The warden shouted, "Listen, you kids! Your mother has rejected you! She doesn't love you!"

She remained in prison for twenty-three more years.

When she was finally released, her son was 34 years old and worked in a government job in Tibet. Sister Yuen had not seen him even once in all those years. He had been taken by the state and raised in atheistic schools, so he had no belief in God and had been told his own mother had forsaken him. Many Christians had visited him and shared the gospel with him, but he always responded by saying, "Your Jesus took my mother away from me, why should I believe in him?"

Upon her release Sister Yuen went to Tibet to find her son. He rejected her, screaming that he had no mother, and pushed her from his home. She has never seen him again.

It is not easy being a disciple.

## Turning Humiliation into a Crown

*Fear of man will prove to be a snare, but whoever trusts in the Lord is kept safe.*

— *Proverbs 29:25*

During the Cultural Revolution Christians were often forced to parade in public wearing a large, cone-shaped dunce's cap with their crimes written on it. These hats were often three feet tall and were very heavy as they were made of bamboo. People would come out to mock the criminals who wore them. But some believers have learned that when they go the extra mile and embrace this pain and humiliation, there is absolutely nothing the world can do to affect them.

This was the case with Brother Shui.

When the time came for Brother Shui to be paraded in public, the police could not find a dunce's cap for him, so they made him walk without one. This upset him deeply, for he wanted to wear a cap proclaiming his crime: "This person believes in Jesus." Many believers took this label as a badge of pride, rather than humiliation. The words were also a witness to unbelievers, who could clearly see the peace and joy on the faces of the believers when they compared them to the other criminals.

Brother Shui cried out in deep anguish, "O Lord, why did you forget me?"

On the second day a dunce's cap was found for Brother Shui. He was delighted! His face shone with joy as he paraded through the streets, now considered worthy to suffer fully for the name of the Lord. Other Christians gained much strength when they saw the joy of the Lord on the face of Brother Shui.

After the parade Brother Shui asked the police if he could keep the cap and take it home when he was released from the prison as a souvenir and a reminder of his "crimes." The police found this request very strange, but they consented.

After his release, Brother Shui returned to his farm. Much to the amazement of his neighbors, he was seen wearing the dunce's cap while he worked out in the fields! Many people thought he had lost his mind, or that he was a shameless man. They despised him. But Brother Shui was a simple man who loved Jesus with all his heart.

The government was infuriated when they saw Brother Shui embracing what was meant to be his humiliation. They realized they could do nothing to make him change his ways or renounce his Lord.

The world can do nothing to someone who has no fear of other people.

It has rightly been stated, "If you haven't discovered something you are willing to die for, then you haven't yet found anything worth living for."

Have you found something worth dying for yet?

# 11

# Sleeping Church, Awake!

*He who gathers crops in summer is a wise son, but he who sleeps during harvest is a disgraceful son.*

— Proverbs 10:5

*A sluggard does not plow in season; so at harvest time he looks but finds nothing.*

— Proverbs 20:4

The world is lost! The Bible declares all of mankind to be spiritually dead, and a dead corpse cannot help but stink! The people of the world are drowning in an ocean of sin and wickedness. If they don't hear the gospel in their lifetime, then they are destined for an eternity of punishment in hell. The only way they will hear that Jesus had made a way for them to escape this dreadful destiny is if we tell them! Many Christians somehow think it is someone else's responsibility to tell the lost about Jesus. We make up numerous excuses to try to justify our inactivity and ease our consciences, but the Lord knows the truth,

> *Rescue those being led away to death; hold back those staggering towards slaughter. If you say, "But we knew nothing about this," does not he who weighs the heart perceive it? Does not he who guards your life know it? Will he not repay each person according to what he has done? (Prov. 24: 11–12)*

The time is short, and it will not do for Christians to continue to play games while millions of people around us are perishing and going to hell.

William Booth, the founder of the Salvation Army, was used mightily by God in the 1800s. He once had a powerful vision from the Lord as he traveled on a train in England. That vision changed Booth's life forever. Let us pay careful attention to his words, and examine our own hearts to see whether we are active participants in the work of God's kingdom—or whether we have deceived ourselves into being mere spectators:

I saw a dark and stormy ocean. Over it the black clouds hung heavily; through them every now and then vivid lightning flashed and loud thunder rolled, while the winds moaned, and the waves rose and foamed, towered and broke . . . In that ocean I thought I saw myriads of poor human beings plunging and floating, shouting and shrieking, cursing and struggling and drowning; and as they cursed and screamed they rose and shrieked again, and then some sank to rise no more.

I saw out of this dark angry ocean a mighty rock that rose up with its summit towering high above the black clouds that overhung the stormy sea. All around the base of this great rock I saw a vast platform. Onto this platform, I saw with delight a number of the poor struggling, drowning wretches continually climbing out of the angry ocean.

I saw that a few of those who were already safe on the platform were helping the poor creatures still in the angry waters to reach the place of safety. On looking more closely I found a number of those who had been rescued, industriously working and scheming by ladders, ropes, boats and other means more effective, to deliver the poor strugglers out of the sea. Here and there were some who actually jumped into the water, regardless of the consequences in their passion to "rescue the perishing." And I hardly know which gladdened me the most—the sight of the poor drowning people climbing onto the rocks reaching a place of safety, or the devotion and self-sacrifice of those whose whole being was wrapped up in the effort for their deliverance.

As I looked on, I saw that the occupants of that platform were quite a mixed company. That is, they were divided into different "sets" or classes, and they occupied themselves with different pleasures and employments. But only a very few of them seemed to make it their business to get the people out of the sea. What puzzled me most was the fact that though all of them had been rescued at one time or another from the ocean, nearly everyone seemed to have forgotten all about it. Anyway, it seemed the memory of its darkness and danger no longer troubled them at all. And what seemed equally strange and perplexing to me was that these people did not even seem to have any care—that is, any agonizing care—about the poor perishing ones who were struggling and drowning right before their very eyes . . . many of whom were their own husbands and wives, brothers and sisters and even their own children.

Now this astonishing unconcern could not have been the result of ignorance or lack of knowledge, because they lived right there in full sight of it all and even talked about it sometimes. Many even went regularly to hear lectures and sermons in which the awful state of these poor drowning creatures was described.

The occupants of this platform were engaged in different pursuits and pastimes. Some of them were absorbed day and night in trading and business in order to make gain, storing up their savings in boxes, safes and the like. Many spent their time in amusing themselves with growing flowers on the side of the rock, others in painting pieces of cloth or in playing music, or in dressing themselves up in different styles and walking about to be admired. Some occupied themselves chiefly in eating and drinking, others were taken up with arguing about the poor drowning creatures that had already been rescued. ... And so the multitude went on right before them struggling and shrieking and drowning in the darkness.

Then I saw something that seemed to me even stranger than anything that had gone on before in this strange vision. I saw that some of these people on the platform whom this Wonderful Being had called to, wanting them to come and help Him in His difficult task of saving these perishing creatures, were always praying and crying out to Him to come to them! Some wanted Him to come and stay with them, and spend His time and strength in making them happier. Others wanted Him to come and take away various doubts and misgivings they had concerning the truth of some letters he had written them. Some wanted Him to come and make them feel more secure on the rock—so secure that they would be quite sure that they should never slip off again into the ocean. Numbers of others wanted Him to make them feel quite certain that they would really get off the rock and onto the mainland someday: because as a matter of fact, it was well known that some had walked so carelessly as to lose their footing, and had fallen back again into the stormy waters.

So these people used to meet and get up as high on the rock as they could, and looking towards the mainland (where they thought the Great Being was) they would cry out, "Come to us! Come and help us!" And all the while he was down (by His Spirit) among the poor struggling, drowning creatures in the angry deep, with His arms around them trying to drag them out, and looking up—oh! so longingly but all in vain—to those on the rock, crying to them with His voice all hoarse from calling, "Come to Me! Come, and help Me!"

And then I understood it all. It was plain enough. The sea was the ocean of life—the sea of real, actual human existence. That lightning was the gleaming of piercing truth coming from Jehovah's Throne. That thunder was the distant echoing of the wrath of God. Those multitudes of people shrieking, struggling, and agonizing in the stormy sea, was the thousands and thousands of poor harlots and harlot-makers, of drunkards and drunkard-makers, of thieves, liars, blasphemers and ungodly people of every kindred, tongue and nation. . . .

The handful of fierce, determined ones, who were risking their own lives in saving the perishing were true soldiers of the cross of Jesus. That Mighty Being who was calling to them from the midst of the angry waters was the Son of God, "the same yesterday, today, and forever" who is still struggling and interceding to save the dying multitudes about us from this terrible doom of damnation, and whose voice can be heard above the music, machinery, and noise of life, calling on the rescued to come and help Him save the world.

My friends in Christ, you are rescued from the waters, you are on the rock, He is in the dark sea calling on you to come to Him and help Him. Will you go? Look for yourselves. The surging sea of life, crowded with perishing multitudes rolls up to the very spot on which you stand.

Leaving the vision, I now come to speak of the fact—a fact that is as real as the Bible, as real as the Christ who hung upon the cross, as real as the judgment day will be, and as real as the heaven and hell that will follow it. Look! Don't be deceived by appearances—men and things are not what they seem. All who are not on the rock are in the sea! Look at them from the standpoint of the great White Throne, and what a sight you have! Jesus Christ, the Son of God is, through His Spirit, in the midst of this dying multitude, struggling to save them. And he is calling on you to jump into the sea—to go right away to His side and help Him in the holy strife. Will you jump? That is, will you go to His feet and place yourself absolutely at His disposal? [41]

To be a Christian and have only a lukewarm, passionless heart for Christ and the souls of lost men and women is a terrible indictment. Millions of people die without knowing Jesus because the Christians they came into contact with couldn't be bothered to be *"prepared to give an answer to everyone who asks you to give the reason for the hope that you have"* (1 Pet. 3:15).

Jesus even suggests that people suffering eternal torment in hell have more passion for evangelism than many Christians! He told a parable about a rich man and Lazarus. The rich man, suffering in agony in the flames of hell, called out across a great chasm to Abraham, *"I beg you, father, send Lazarus to my father's house, for I have five brothers. Let him warn them, so that they will not also come to this place of torment"* (Luke 16:27).

If people in hell strongly desire to reach the lost, shouldn't we who are called by the Name of the Lord be even more committed to this task?

God cannot use a person who wants a safe and comfortable Christian life. If your only aim in life is to get yourself to heaven, then you are not likely to take many other people with you. Many Christians have somehow become deceived into spiritual selfishness, gorging themselves on the latest Christian teaching, books, seminars, music, and fads. When we spend all our time edifying ourselves and not seeking to win the souls of lost humanity, we are in deep trouble! Ironically, the more we feed our souls without serving God's purposes in the earth, the more our souls get sick of the food and bloated with information. This is why the Scripture says, *"He who is full loathes honey; but to the hungry even what is bitter tastes sweet"* (Prov. 27:7).

The Dead Sea in Israel serves as an excellent example of what can happen to a believer, a church, or even a whole nation that is self-absorbed. The Dead Sea is aptly named, as it is full of salt and contains few living creatures. Yet a closer inspection reveals that it has 153 sources of fresh water flowing into it. Numerous rivers (including the famous Jordan), streams and creeks flow into the Dead Sea, carrying fish and other aquatic life.

Yet once the fresh water reaches the Dead Sea the fish die and the water starts to stink. Why do the fish and other forms of life die? Simply because the Dead Sea has no outlet. It is constantly taking in but never giving out. The water stagnates and salts up. Life turns to death, freshness to salty sludge.

Christian, beware! You must have an outlet for your faith or your spiritual life will stagnate and begin to stink! Pastor, be warned. You will be held responsible before God not only for what you feed his sheep, but for what form of outreach you lead them into. Are new souls being birthed in your church on a regular basis? If not, you are stagnating. You must find an effective outlet for your faith, not only to expand God's kingdom among the lost but also to focus the vision of the believers and bring life to your congregation.

When Christians are regularly engaged in genuine outreach, they will be giving out and not only taking in, so they will need more spiritual nourishment in order to replace what they gave away. There will be a spiritual flow, in and out, and the cobwebs and spiritual disease that can easily riddle believers' lives will be washed away. When people are focused on the needs of others, there is little opportunity for them to sit around complaining, gossiping, and slandering each other. Instead of criticizing your sermons, people will start to obey God's word and will themselves become a living sermon to the world. The Bible will stop being a book of knowledge and will become a book of life.

The same holds true for prayer. It, too, needs to be outward focused. It is a spiritual principle that people who only pray for themselves and their own personal needs will never change. But when they intercede on behalf of other people, God will change their hearts as they pray. The best way for a selfish person to be delivered from self-obsession is to start praying for and meeting the needs of others.

The church in China is not focused on evangelism merely because it an activity of the church. Evangelism is for the glory of God. It is the reason we exist on this earth; it is our main act of worship. Worship is far more than just the singing of songs. Worship occurs every time a believer does something that brings honor and glory to Jesus.

If God's only goal were to get people into heaven, then he would take us there as soon as we first believed in him. However, he chooses to leave us in this world so that our lives and words can witness for Jesus Christ to all of humanity. When we witness, not as works but because we love Jesus and want to see his name glorified, our spiritual lives will be strong, as will our love of God's word. No hardship or persecution will dampen our hunger for the Lord, for *"to the hungry even what is bitter tastes great."*

In so many ways God's principles are the exact opposite of how we humans think. Often we think that if we edify ourselves enough, then we will be spiritually satisfied, when actually fulfilment comes when we serve God through serving the needs of mankind. This is the explanation of the Apostle Paul's words to Philemon: *"I pray that you may be active in sharing your faith, so that you will have a full understanding of every good thing we have in Christ"*(Phil. 6).

Have you ever wondered why some churches have a problem with lukewarm, backslidden Christians? We have found that backsliding is mostly due to a lack of witnessing for the Lord. Pastors often think people backslide because they cannot hold onto certain theological truths, but the problem is usually disobedience, not theology. The longer a person disobeys God, the colder their heart grows. The gospel is a gospel of action, not a gospel of self-preservation. The pursuit of doctrinal purity in and of itself only results in legalistic bondage if you have no intention of also obeying God's command to proclaim the gospel throughout the earth.

Christians, if you have truly been saved, don't be ashamed to get busy for the Lord! There are multitudes of souls perishing all around you. If you don't go and reach them, who will? *"How, then, can they call on the one they have not believed in? And how can they believe in the one of whom they have not heard? And how can they hear without someone preaching to them?"*(Rom. 10:14).

Don't be discouraged when the devil sends people along who try to stop you or persuade you to wait until you are "more mature." If we wait until we are perfect before we serve God, we will be waiting until Jesus returns.

A good church leader is someone who spends lots of time with the Lord and receives direction from the word of God to guide the church. The leaders should be the ones who cast the vision before the people, calling them to join in the work of the Lord. The leader needs to be full of love and mercy, but also strong and confident, for *"if the trumpet does not sound a clear call, who will get ready for battle?"* (1 Cor. 14:8).

All through the Scriptures—whether we study the life of Moses, David, Jeremiah, John the Baptist, Peter, or Paul—God's leaders were people who sounded a clear trumpet call. The people respected the hand of God on their lives and willingly followed the vision set before them.

Pastor, your primary responsibility is to give spiritual direction and leadership to the flock God has entrusted to your care. In China we believe the shepherd should be out in front of the flock, leading them through dangerous places. The willing sheep follow behind.

Too many times, however, the shepherd of a church is not leading from the front but is at the back of the flock, trying to encourage the weakest and most nervous sheep to inch their way forward. This kind of leadership will never achieve anything! You will spend all your time in counseling sessions and dealing with the problems in your congregation! The devil will continually invent more problems just to keep you tied up and away from leading your church into the real battlefield, which is the war for the souls of mankind.

Denominational pride is one of the easiest ways the devil can deceive us. Often our denomination or church thinks it is doing well compared to others. We sit in our boats and closely watch others as they drift further and further from the shore of God's truth. "It's terrible how they have drifted into error," we say, not noticing that we, too, have slowly drifted away from the shore while our attention has been focused on our pitiful neighbors.

Whole churches and denominations have drifted into dangerous territory without any realization of it. The answer to staying rooted in the Lord is to stop comparing ourselves with others and compare ourselves with the Lord Jesus instead. When we compare ourselves with others, we usually feel pretty good about ourselves. When we compare ourselves with Jesus, we see we are wretched and naked and we throw ourselves at the feet of the Lord, asking for mercy. This is how God intended us to live, in daily reliance on him for our existence. *"If anyone thinks he is something when he is nothing, he deceives himself. Each one should test his own actions ... without comparing himself to somebody else"* (Gal. 6:3–4).

Christians all around the world use Revelation 3:20 as an invitation to salvation, *"Here I am! I stand at the door and knock. If anyone hears my voice and opens the door, I will come in and eat with him, and he with me."* But closer examination of this passage reveals that Jesus wasn't knocking at the door of unbelievers' hearts when he said those words. He was knocking at the door of the backslidden church at Laodicea! Jesus was standing outside the door of the church, knocking and asking to be let in! What a sad indictment that Jesus is an unwelcome guest in many churches today. Many continue to operate in their lifeless religiosity, *"having a form of godliness, but denying its power"* (2 Tim. 3:5).

Wake up! Repent! Let God come into your lives and into your churches. He loves all people and as long as you have breath in you it's not too late for him to use you for his glory.

A spiritually dull church or believer is a poor witness for the living, resurrected Jesus.

A church is meant to be a training center and command hub for war, not a social club for pleasantries and hypocrisy, where people give lip service to Christ while refusing to obey his commands.

It's time to wake up!

What should you and your church do if you have been sleeping and neglecting God's work? The answer is clearly found in the words of Jesus to the lukewarm church: *"Wake up! Strengthen what remains and is about to die, for I have not found your deeds complete in the sight of my God. Remember, therefore, what you have received and heard, obey it; and repent. But if you do not wake up, I will come like a thief, and you will not know at what time I will come to you"* (Rev. 3:2–3).

# 12

# Fishing Lessons

*Simon Peter climbed aboard and dragged the net ashore. It was full of large fish, 153, but even with so many the net was not torn.*

— *John 21:11*

The word of God is full of encouragement and lessons for those with a teachable heart and an ear to hear what the Holy Spirit is saying to them.

Many people hear God's voice calling them to catch fish for the kingdom of God. The disciples heard Jesus say, *"Let's go over to the other side."* They then rowed out onto the lake, taking *"him along, just as he was, in the boat"* (Mark 4:35–36). Jesus was soon asleep, and a fierce storm arose.

As you launch into your ministry, make sure Jesus isn't asleep in your boat! You can try to row your boat or operate your ministry in your own strength, but you'll not get far while Jesus is sleeping. The disciples found that *"the waves broke over the boat, so that it was nearly swamped"* (v. 37). Wake Jesus up and make him the Lord and Master of everything you do! Too many churches and ministries have welcomed Jesus into their midst in the past, but today they are operating in their own strength and their own plans while Jesus sleeps in their midst.

\* \* \*

On an earlier occasion, when Jesus first met Andrew and Peter, he said, *"Come, follow me . . . and I will make you fishers of men"* (Mark 1:17).

God wants all Christians to be fishers of men. The world is in a desperate, destructive mess. Nations wage war on each other, and every day people inflict unmentionable cruelty on one another. If we have Jesus in our hearts, we are called to be fishermen, regardless of our background, education, or economic position. Some individuals may be more gifted at fishing than we are, but we can never excuse ourselves from the personal responsibility we have to reach out to the lost. We can trick ourselves, and maybe even other people, but we can never deceive the Lord. Each Christian will one day give an account of the way they used, or didn't use, the talents God gave them.

It is time to commit ourselves fully to the cause of God, without reservation. If you do this you will not fail to experience the blessing and presence of God in a sweet and powerful way.

One day Jesus saw some fishermen by the Lake of Gennesaret who had pulled their nets up and were washing them (Luke 5:2). Washing our fishing nets from time to time is necessary if we constantly use them to catch fish, but today many churches have become professional net washers. Instead of catching souls for the kingdom of God, they spend all their time talking about fishing, studying various fishing strategies and techniques, listening to the lectures of fishing experts, and singing songs about fishing. Yet they rarely, or never, actually go fishing!

Many pastors fill their pulpits with fishing stories, and their congregation admires the fishing nets that hang on the wall of the church for display. The nets have been thoroughly cleaned. No effort has been spared to keep all dirt and impurity out of the church. The nets have been bleached so white that nobody would ever guess they had once been used for fishing! The strings are carefully arranged so that each square has the same size and shape. After all, "God is a God of order." The pastors love to boast about their nets, and even invite Christians from other churches to come and admire their nets with them.

Every few years "over-zealous" young believers come in and suggest that they should take the nets down from the wall and take them out on the lake to catch fish. The "mature" members of the congregation explain that God is catching many fish throughout the world, and all is well. Their job is to live holy, peaceful lives and not be presumptuous. The new believers are assured that once they have followed the Lord for a few more years, they will mature and become just like the others. For now, they had best remain quiet in the pew and stop speaking out of turn.

Week after week, year after year, Satan lulls individual believers, churches, and whole denominations to sleep with his lies. The bleach that has removed all the stains and dirt from the nets also effectively disinfects the Christians until they will never consider becoming fishermen again.

After teaching the people from Peter's boat a little way from the shore, Jesus said, *"Put out into deep water, and let down the nets for a catch."* Peter was reluctant to go out again. He must have been exhausted after the night's efforts had failed to bring in even a single fish. He said, *"Master, we've worked hard all night and haven't caught anything. But because you say so, I will let down the nets"* (Luke 5:4–5:5).

Christian, do you feel like Peter did? Have you convinced yourself that there are no more fish left in the sea? Have your church programs failed to net any new fish for so long that you would rather stay on the bank washing your nets, because one more failed fishing trip might be more than you can take? Many churches have given up on evangelism because they "tried it, and it didn't work."

Please don't deceive yourself into thinking there are no more fish left in the sea! We have heard statements like "Nobody around here is interested in the gospel any more." This is a lie from Satan. There are plenty of fish left in the sea. The problem is never a lack of fish. The problem may be us and our ineffective fishing techniques! Perhaps our nets have not even been in the water!

Peter caught nothing while he and his friends operated in their own strength. They were convinced there were no fish left. But when they gave up and allowed God to direct their efforts, suddenly *"they caught such a large number of fish that their nets began to break"* (Luke 5:6).

Please understand this! When we try to serve the Lord and preach the gospel in our own strength, using our own programs and initiatives, we will fail and will soon convince ourselves the problem lies not with us, but with the "apathetic heathens" who "show no interest in the gospel." But when we learn what it truly means to give ourselves to God unreservedly, asking him to fill and empower us, we will start to be in a place where God can use us for his glory. As long as you are looking for God to bless "your" ministry, you are wasting time. He only blesses his ministry, done his way, by his leading. When we finally reach the end of all our useless programs and give up in desperation, Jesus will always be there to show us a better way—his way. He will tell us where to throw our nets and we will be amazed to see our nets bulging with fish.

We should never forget that the Bible talks of those who know Jesus as alive and those who don't as dead. We tend to view people as good and bad, but to God the issue is always one of life and death.

It should be little wonder that our worldly evangelism programs fail to gain the attention of the spiritually dead people all around us. It's only when Jesus starts to speak deep into people's hearts that their dead spirits can awake to eternal life.

Where were the fish when Peter was trying to catch them all night? They were right there in the darkness of the water, unseen by Peter and his companions. They easily avoided the nets set for them. But the next morning Jesus, the Creator of the world, knew exactly where each fish was. He made each one of them. Imagine how excited those little fish must have been to hear the voice of their Creator. Maybe they came closer to the surface to catch a glimpse of the Lord of Heaven! In China we have seen the hardest sinners fall to their knees in repentance when they came face to face with Jesus. We have seen numerous murderers, rapists, and prostitutes caught up in God's net because they heard the voice of Jesus calling them.

Pastors, your church must get busy fishing because this is what the church is meant to do. Jesus never intended his people to become insular and just sit around edifying each other. It is also not the job of a leader to spend all his time dealing with problems in the church. Of course there will always be problems until Jesus returns, but they should not bog you down. Instead, you should see them as opportunities to mend your net so that you can go fishing for souls with a stronger net.

The devil will send all kinds of problems to distract you from fishing, so you need a firm and unwavering focus to win souls. Has your church given up trying to catch fish? Have you been busy cleaning your nets, convinced that there are no more fish left in the sea? The Bible has some exciting news for you! Not only does God want to change you and empower your ministry, but after he does so you will be a tremendous example for many others to follow. After Peter's nets began to break because of the weight of the full nets, *"they signaled their partners in the other boat to come and help them, and they came and filled both boats so full that they began to sink"* (Luke 5:7).

It was at this stage that Peter realized his own complete sinfulness, and the futility of his flesh. He *"fell at Jesus' knees and said, 'Go away from me, Lord; I am a sinful man'"* (Luke 5:8).

Jesus didn't contradict Peter's statement. We all need to realize we are sinful, and that *"all of us have become like one who is unclean, and all our righteous acts are like filthy rags; we all shrivel up like a leaf, and like the wind our sins sweep us away"* (Isa. 64:6).

Instead, Jesus said to Peter, *"'Don't be afraid; from now on you will catch men.' So they pulled their boats up on shore, left everything and followed him"* (Luke 5:11–12).

Are you also willing to let Jesus take control of you and make you a fisher of men's souls?

# 13

# The Nations in the Back to Jerusalem Vision

The following list includes all fifty-one countries lying within the 10/40 window that are less than 5 percent Christian. In some cases, such as Brunei, Bahrain, and Kuwait, the total Christian population is higher than 5 percent but special circumstances warrant the inclusion of these countries. In Bahrain and Kuwait most of the Christians are foreign expatriates, while in Brunei almost all of the believers are Chinese and there is not a single known Christian among the Malay majority.

The list is not intended to be definitive for the Back to Jerusalem movement. Chinese missionaries go wherever the Lord leads them, including to some countries not on this list. Some feel called to the Caucasus Republics in Russia, for example, where sixty Muslim people groups live without the gospel. Others are called to countries like Malaysia and Indonesia, where the church is strong among the Chinese but small among the tens of millions of non-Chinese.[42]

## NORTH ASIA

| Japan | |
|---|---|
| Population: | 127 million |
| Capital: | Tokyo |
| People groups: | 34 |
| Main religion: | Buddhism/Shintoism 70% |
| All Christians: | 1.5% |

| Mongolia | |
|---|---|
| Population: | 2.8 million |
| Capital: | Ulan Bator |
| People groups: | 20 |
| Main religion: | Buddhism/Shamanism 54% |
| All Christians: | 0.7% |

| North Korea | |
|---|---|
| Population: | 25.5 million |
| Capital: | Pyongyang |
| People groups: | 6 |
| Main religion: | Atheist 64% |
| All Christians: | 1.6% |

# SOUTHEAST ASIA

| Brunei | |
|---|---|
| Population: | 358,000 |
| Capital: | Bandar Seri Begawan |
| People groups: | 29 |
| Main religion: | Islam 65% |
| All Christians: | 11% (almost all Chinese) |

| Cambodia | |
|---|---|
| Population: | 11.9 million |
| Capital: | Phnom Penh |
| People groups: | 46 |
| Main religion: | Buddhism 83% |
| All Christians: | 1.2% |

| Laos | |
|---|---|
| Population: | 6.4 million |
| Capital: | Vientiane |
| People groups: | 145 |
| Main religion: | Buddhism 61% |
| All Christians: | 1.8% |

| Myanmar (Burma) | |
|---|---|
| Population: | 48 million |
| Capital: | Yangon (Rangoon) |
| People groups: | 135 |
| Main religion: | Buddhism 83% |
| All Christians: | 8% (mostly ethnic minorities) |

| Thailand | |
|---|---|
| Population: | 63 million |
| Capital: | Bangkok |
| People groups: | 101 |
| Main religion: | Buddhism 93% |
| All Christians: | 1.6% |

# SOUTH ASIA

| Bangladesh | |
|---|---|
| Population: | 138 million |
| Capital: | Dhaka |
| People groups: | 61 |
| Main religion: | Islam 86% |
| All Christians: | 0.7% |

| Bhutan | |
|---|---|
| Population: | 2.2 million |
| Capital: | Thimpu |
| People groups: | 20 |
| Main religion: | Buddhism 72% |
| All Christians: | 0.4% |

| India | |
|---|---|
| Population: | 1,048 million |
| Capital: | New Delhi |
| People groups: | 2,329 |
| Main religion: | Hinduism 80% |
| All Christians: | 4% |

| Maldives | |
|---|---|
| Population: | 321,000 |
| Capital: | Male |
| People groups: | 8 |
| Main religion: | Islam 99.5% |
| All Christians: | 0.1% |

| Nepal | |
|---|---|
| Population: | 25.9 million |
| Capital: | Kathmandu |
| People groups: | 130 |
| Main religion: | Hinduism 75% |
| All Christians: | 1.9% |

## CENTRAL ASIA

| Afghanistan | |
|---|---|
| Population: | 27.9 million |
| Capital: | Kabul |
| People groups: | 91 |
| Main religion: | Islam 98% |
| All Christians: | 0.02% |

| Azerbaijan | |
|---|---|
| Population: | 7.8 million |
| Capital: | Baku |
| People groups: | 39 |
| Main religion: | Islam 84% |
| All Christians: | 4.6% |

| Kazakhstan | |
|---|---|
| Population: | 16.7 million |
| Capital: | Astana |
| People groups: | 54 |
| Main religion: | Islam 61% |
| All Christians: | 24% (mostly Russians) |

| Kyrgyzstan | |
|---|---|
| Population: | 4.8 million |
| Capital: | Bishkek |
| People groups: | 45 |
| Main religion: | Islam 78% |
| All Christians: | 7% (mostly Russians) |

| Pakistan | |
|---|---|
| Population: | 158 million |
| Capital: | Islamabad |
| People groups: | 488 |
| Main religion: | Islam 96% |
| All Christians: | 2.3% |

| Tajikistan | |
|---|---|
| Population: | 6.7 million |
| Capital: | Dushanbe |
| People groups: | 46 |
| Main religion: | Islam 90% |
| All Christians: | 1.4% |

| Turkmenistan | |
|---|---|
| Population: | 4.7 million |
| Capital: | Ashgabat |
| People groups: | 42 |
| Main religion: | Islam 92% |
| All Christians: | 2.6% (mostly Russians) |

| Uzbekistan | |
|---|---|
| Population: | 25.6 million |
| Capital: | Tashkent |
| People groups: | 66 |
| Main religion: | Islam 84% |
| All Christians: | 1.2% (mostly Russians) |

# THE MIDDLE EAST

| Bahrain | |
|---|---|
| Population: | 758,000 |
| Capital: | Manama |
| People groups: | 15 |
| Main religion: | Islam 82% |
| All Christians: | Christian 10% (mostly foreigners) |

| Iran | |
|---|---|
| Population: | 70.6 million |
| Capital: | Tehran |
| People groups: | 109 |
| Main religion: | Islam 99% |
| All Christians: | 0.3% |

| Iraq | |
|---|---|
| Population: | 24.1 million |
| Capital: | Baghdad |
| People groups: | 42 |
| Main religion: | Islam 97% |
| All Christians: | 1.5% |

| Israel | |
|---|---|
| Population: | 6 million |
| Capital: | Jerusalem |
| People groups: | 57 |
| Main religion: | Judaism 81% |
| All Christians: | 2% |

| Jordan | |
|---|---|
| Population: | 7.7 million |
| Capital: | Amman |
| People groups: | 22 |
| Main religion: | Islam 96% |
| All Christians: | 2.7% |

| Kuwait | |
|---|---|
| Population: | 2.1 million |
| Capital: | Kuwait City |
| People groups: | 34 |
| Main religion: | Islam 87% |
| All Christians: | 8% (mostly foreigners) |

| Oman | |
|---|---|
| Population: | 2.7 million |
| Capital: | Muscat |
| People groups: | 39 |
| Main religion: | Islam 93% |
| All Christians: | 2.5% |

| Palestine | |
|---|---|
| Population: | 3.9 million |
| Capital: | Gaza (Jerusalem is claimed) |
| People groups: | 21 |
| Main religion: | Islam 87% |
| All Christians: | 1.9% |

| Qatar | |
|---|---|
| Population: | 752,000 |
| Capital: | Doha |
| People groups: | 25 |
| Main religion: | Islam 80% |
| All Christians: | 10% (mostly foreigners) |

| Saudi Arabia | |
|---|---|
| Population: | 23.6 million |
| Capital: | Riyadh |
| People groups: | 45 |
| Main religion: | Islam 93% |
| All Christians: | 4% (mostly foreigners) |

| Syria | |
|---|---|
| Population: | 17.2 million |
| Capital: | Damascus |
| People groups: | 36 |
| Main religion: | Islam 91% |
| All Christians: | 5% |

| Turkey | |
|---|---|
| Population: | 69 million |
| Capital: | Ankara |
| People groups: | 66 |
| Main religion: | Islam 99.6% |
| All Christians: | 0.3% |

| United Arab Emirates | |
|---|---|
| Population: | 2.6 million |
| Capital: | Abu Dhabi |
| People groups: | 54 |
| Main religion: | Islam 66% |
| All Christians: | 9% (mostly foreigners) |

| Yemen | |
|---|---|
| Population: | 18.8 million |
| Capital: | Sana'a |
| People groups: | 30 |
| Main religion: | Islam 99.94% |
| All Christians: | 0.05% |

# NORTH AFRICA

| Algeria | |
|---|---|
| Population: | 32.3 million |
| Capital: | Algiers |
| People groups: | 51 |
| Main religion: | Islam 97% |
| All Christians: | 0.3% |

| Comoro Islands | |
|---|---|
| Population: | 662,000 |
| Capital: | Moroni |
| People groups: | 11 |
| Main religion: | Islam 98% |
| All Christians: | 0.8% |

| Djibouti | |
|---|---|
| Population: | 669,000 |
| Capital: | Djibouti City |
| People groups: | 9 |
| Main religion: | Islam 94% |
| All Christians: | 4.6% |

| Egypt | |
|---|---|
| Population: | 73.8 million |
| Capital: | Cairo |
| People groups: | 40 |
| Main religion: | Islam 87% |
| All Christians: | 12% |

| Gambia | |
|---|---|
| Population: | 1.4 million |
| Capital: | Banjul |
| People groups: | 36 |
| Main religion: | Islam 89% |
| All Christians: | 4% |

| Guinea | |
|---|---|
| Population: | 7.8 million |
| Capital: | Conakry |
| People groups: | 52 |
| Main religion: | Islam 86% |
| All Christians: | 4% |

| Libya | |
|---|---|
| Population: | 6.1 million |
| Capital: | Tripoli |
| People groups: | 42 |
| Main religion: | Islam 97% |
| All Christians: | 3% |

| Mali | |
|---|---|
| Population: | 12.3 million |
| Capital: | Bamako |
| People groups: | 52 |
| Main religion: | Islam 87% |
| All Christians: | 1.9% |

| Mauritania | |
|---|---|
| Population: | 2.8 million |
| Capital: | Nouakchott |
| People groups: | 26 |
| Main religion: | Islam 99.8% |
| All Christians: | 0.2% |

| Morocco | |
|---|---|
| Population: | 31 million |
| Capital: | Rabat |
| People groups: | 33 |
| Main religion: | Islam 99.85% |
| All Christians: | 0.1% |

| Niger | |
|---|---|
| Population: | 10.7 million |
| Capital: | Niamey |
| People groups: | 41 |
| Main religion: | Islam 98% |
| All Christians: | 0.4% |

| Senegal | |
|---|---|
| Population: | 10.6 million |
| Capital: | Dakar |
| People groups: | 58 |
| Main religion: | Islam 92% |
| All Christians: | 4% |

| Somalia | |
|---|---|
| Population: | 11.9 million |
| Capital: | Mogadishu |
| People groups: | 17 |
| Main religion: | Islam 99.95% |
| All Christians: | 0.05% |

| Tunisia | |
|---|---|
| Population: | 9.9 million |
| Capital: | Tunis |
| People groups: | 27 |
| Main religion: | Islam 99.7% |
| All Christians: | 0.2% |

| Western Sahara | |
|---|---|
| Population: | 247,000 |
| Capital: | Laayoune |
| People groups: | 11 |
| Main religion: | Islam 100% |
| All Christians: | 0% |

# SUMMARY OF THE COUNTRIES IN THE BACK TO JERUSALEM VISION

| Region | Countries | Population | People groups | Main religion |
|---|---|---|---|---|
| North Asia | 3 | 155,300,000 | 60 | Buddhism 2, Atheism 1 |
| Southeast Asia | 6 | 213,658,000 | 595 | Buddhism 5, Islam 1 |
| South Asia | 5 | 1,214,721,000 | 2,548 | Hinduism 2, Islam 2, Buddhism 1 |
| Central Asia | 8 | 252,200,000 | 871 | Islam 8 |
| Middle East | 14 | 249,810,000 | 595 | Islam 13, Judaism 1 |
| North Africa | 15 | 212,178,000 | 506 | Islam 15 |
| TOTALS: | 51 | 2,297,867,000 | 5,175 | Islam 39, Buddhism 8, Hinduism 2, Judaism 1, Atheism 1 |

# Notes

[1] Brother Yun with Paul Hattaway, *The Heavenly Man: The Remarkable True Story of Chinese Christian Brother Yun* (London: Monarch Books, 2002), pp. 311–312.

[2] The best of several books on this subject is C. H. Kang & Ethel Nelson, *The Discovery of Genesis* (St.Louis: Concordia Publishing House, 1979).

[3] James Legge, *The Notions of the Chinese Concerning God and Spirits* (Hong Kong Register Office, 1852), pp. 24–28.

[4] www.CL2000.com, "Christian Designs Found in Tomb Stones of Eastern Han Dynasty", 2 August 2002.

[5] Milton T. Stauffer, *The Christian Occupation of China* (Shanghai: Christian Consultation Committee, 1922), p. 161.

[6] Daniel W. Fisher, *Calvin Wilson Mateer: A Biography* (Philadelphia: The Westminster Press, 1911), p. 319.

[7] Theodore Mueller, *Great Missionaries to China* (Grand Rapids: Zondervan, 1947), p. 111.

[8] George Sweeting, *More than 2000 Great Quotes and Illustrations* (Texas: Word Publishing, 1985), p. 184.

[9] F. Howard Taylor, in Andrew Gih, edited by J. Edwin Orr, *Launch Out into the Deep* (London: Marshall, Morgan & Scott, 1938), p. 11.

[10] Hannah Davies, *Among Hills and Valleys in Western China* (London: S. W. Partridge & Co., 1901), p. 270.

[11] Archie R. Crouch, Steven Agoratus, Arthur Emerson and Debra E. Soled (eds.), *Christianity in China: A Scholar's Guide to Resources in the Libraries and Archives of the United States* (New York: M. E. Sharpe, 1989), p. xxxi.

[12] *North China Herald*, 1 June 1888, p. 513.

[13] Brother Yun, *The Heavenly Man*, pp. 20–21.

[14] David H. Adeney, *China: The Church's Long March* (Ventura, Calif.: Regal Books, 1985), p. 206.

[15] Some "China experts" refuse to accept any but the lowest estimates of the number of Christians in China, believing all higher figures to be irresponsible speculation. God willing, I plan to produce a series of books entitled *Fire and Blood* that will examine the church in China province-by-province, giving detailed documentation on the size of the church in every single county and city within each province. The information on which my

figures are based comes from numerous sources, including hundreds of hours of personal interviews with house church leaders responsible for work in every part of China. I started out believing the lower estimates (20 to 35 million Christians in China) to be correct, but have been completely convinced of the existence of 80 to 100+ million believers in China after having been presented with clear and overwhelming statistical evidence of the extent of revival among house churches.

[16] Ibid., pp. 146–165.

[17] Tertullian, *Apology*, chapter 50, A.D. c. 200.

[18] Taken from a little-known 16-page privately published booklet entitled *The Chinese Back-To-Jerusalem Evangelistic Band: A Prayer Call to Christian Friends of the Chinese Church*, 1947.

[19] *Back to Jerusalem*, pp. 3–4. A small prayer booklet with no author, publisher or date listed (probably 1947).

[20] Alice Hayes Taylor, "Back to Jerusalem Evangelistic Band" (unpublished paper, 1948), p. 2.

[21] J. Oswald Sanders, *Seen and Heard in China*, 1948, pp. 38–39.

[22] *The Chinese Back-To-Jerusalem Evangelistic Band*, p. 5.

[23] J. Oswald Sanders, *Seen and Heard in China*, pp. 39–40.

[24] *Back to Jerusalem*, p. 6.

[25] *The Chinese Back-To-Jerusalem Evangelistic Band*, p. 14.

[26] *Back to Jerusalem*, p. 10.

[27] *The Chinese Back-To-Jerusalem Evangelistic Band*, p. 5.

[28] Ibid., p. 8.

[29] Ibid., p. 9.

[30] Ibid., pp. 9-10.

[31] *Back to Jerusalem*, p. 1.

[32] Ibid., p. 14.

[33] J. Oswald Sanders, *Seen and Heard in China*, p. 39.

[34] Alice Taylor, "Back to Jerusalem Evangelistic Band," p. 3.

[35] Ibid., p. 4.

[36] Ibid., p. 5.

[37] Prayer letter of Miss Phyllis Thompson, March 3, 1949; cited in Tony

Lambert, "Back to Jerusalem: Origins of a Missionary Vision (Part II)," *China Insight,* March–April 2003.

[38] Tony Lambert, "Back to Jerusalem: Uncle Simon," *China Insight,* May–June 2003.

[39] Brother Yun, *The Heavenly Man,* p. 240.

[40] Gordon Hickson is currently writing a book, *The Heavenly Virus: Contagious Christian Leadership,* in which he examines this concept in some detail.

[41] The account of Booth's vision has been published in dozens of books and gospel tracts over the years, including several biographies of his life. See Harold Begbie, *Life of William Booth: The Founder of the Salvation Army* (London: Macmillan, 1920, 2 volumes).

[42] The statistics used for the population (2003) and the number of people groups in each country comes from the latest data released by the Joshua Project II. The figures for religious affiliation and Christianity come from Patrick Johnstone & Jason Mandryk with Robyn Johnstone, *Operation World: 21st Century Edition* (Carlisle: Paternoster, 2001).

If you would like ongoing information about the Back to Jerusalem movement, with prayer requests, latest news, and ways you can be involved, please log on to the BTJ website: **www.backtojerusalem.com**

Or write to:
Back to Jerusalem
P.O. Box 23132
91230 Jerusalem
ISRAEL

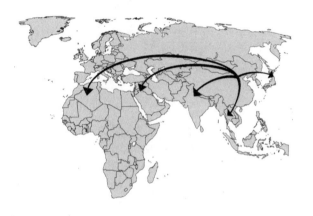

*Paul Hattaway* is the director of Asia Harvest, a Christian ministry committed to serving the Chinese church and the Back to Jerusalem vision:
**www.asiaharvest.org**

# Other books available from...

Gabriel
Resources

PO Box 1047
129 Mobilization Dr
Waynesboro, GA 30830

706-554-1594
1-8MORE-BOOKS
gabriel@omlit.om.org

# Operation World
### and
## Window on the World

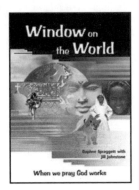

"One way to personally obey the Great Commission is to read the information Operation World so clearly lays out. I have found Operation World to be an effective tool for my own personal life in prayer, and in the presentation of God's Word to the world."

**— Anne Graham Lotz**
AnGeL Ministries

"...the most powerful tool in communicating the development of the evangelical movement as a world-wide phenomenon..."

**— Dwight Gibson**
North American Director of
the World Evangelical Alliance

# Operation World
## 21st Century Edition
Patrick Johnstone & Jason Mandryk

Operation World—the definitive prayer handbook for the church—is now available in its 21st century edition containing 80% new material. Packed with informative and inspiring fuel for prayer about every country of the world, it is essential for anybody who wants to make a difference.

Winner of the 2002 Gold Medallion Book Award for Missions and Evangelism.

1-850783-57-8      810 Pages

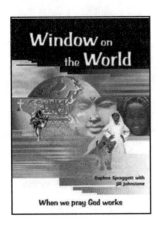

# Window on the World
Daphne Spraggett & Jill Johnstone

A book that will inform and inspire the whole family, this beautifully presented yet practical book is the ideal accompaniment to Operation World. Stunning photographic visuals complement this A–Z of 100 countries and people groups providing an exciting learning experience and guide for prayer.

Winner of the 2002 Gold Medallion Book Award for Elementary Age Children.

1-850783-58-6     221 Pages

# CD ROM

The Operation World CD-ROM goes beyond the text to access Operation World databases and links to websites and numerous other resources. Use this resource to further your own prayer and study of each country. Formatted for both PC and Mac computer systems.

OPW16        810 Pages

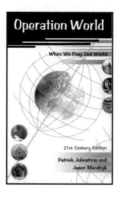 

## Operation World & CD-ROM
### 1-850783-59-4

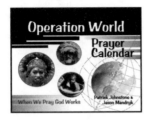

# Prayer Calendar

This spiral desk calendar contains clear graphics and useful geographic, cultural, economic, and political statistics on 122 countries of the world. The *Operation World Prayer Calendar* is a great tool to help you pray intelligently for the world. Pray for each country for three days and see how God works!

1-884543-59-6      256 Pages

# Wall Map
22" x 36"

This beautiful, full-color wall map is a great way to locate the countries that you are praying for each day and build a global picture. Not only an excellent resource for schools, churches, and offices, but a valuable tool for the home.

1-884543-60-X      Laminated
1-884543-61-8      Folded